GILES TERERA

HAMILTON
AND ME
AN ACTOR'S JOURNAL

FOREWORD BY LIN-MANUEL MIRANDA

NICK HERN BOOKS
London
www.nickhernbooks.co.uk

A NICK HERN BOOK

Hamilton and Me
first published in Great Britain in 2021
by Nick Hern Books Limited, The Glasshouse,
49a Goldhawk Road, London W12 8QP

Copyright © 2021 Giles Terera
Foreword copyright © 2021 Lin-Manuel Miranda

All songs lyrics by Lin-Manuel Miranda
© 5000 Broadway Music (ASCAP),
administered by WB Music Corp.

Designed and typeset by Nick Hern Books, London
Printed and bound in UK by
CPI Group (Ltd), Croydon, CR0 4YY

A CIP catalogue record for this book
is available from the British Library

ISBN 978 1 84842 999 4

For my mother and
Reba Younge, who guided me
Claudette Williams, who taught me
Hilary Gagan, who believed in me
Nettie Battam, who inspired me
and Katy Bryant,
our *Hamilton* company manager,
who helped me more than words can say.

'Had I read Sterne more and Voltaire less, I should have known the world was wide enough for Hamilton and me.'

Aaron Burr

CONTENTS

FOREWORD

I was lucky enough to be in the room where it happened: Giles Terera's audition for *Hamilton*.

Serendipity was at play here—because for ninety per cent of the actors we hired for the West End production of *Hamilton*, I had to settle for watching tapes of their auditions from my home in New York.

But I just so happened to be rehearsing for *Mary Poppins Returns* in London that fall. And I just so happened to come down with a severe inner-ear infection the week before. The kind that sets the horizon wobbling and your innate sense of balance reeling.

Having no fixed horizon, and temporary vertigo makes dancing very difficult, I skipped dance rehearsals for the film and went to *Hamilton* auditions instead. As long as I kept my head absolutely level, I was alright. That's how I happened to be in the room to see Giles.

What struck me as soon as Giles launched into 'Wait for It' was the *clarity* of his storytelling: as he sang the first verse, relating Burr's romantic travails, I felt as if I were hearing this story for the very first time. Maybe it's all that Shakespearean training, but Giles loves language and storytelling. Most musical theatre actors try to show you what a beautiful voice they have in their short time in the audition room; Giles came in with a laser focus on the story and the words. To hear a song you've written and experience it as if you are hearing it for the first time is quite a feat. I knew a world-class talent was in front of me.

That's also what you have in front of you in this book, one of the most joyous and clear-eyed approaches to playing a character that I have ever read. Watching Giles pull together his *own* Aaron Burr (as the great Leslie Odom Jr. did alongside me in the United States when he originated the role), you get to witness a world-class talent at work. You'll see what he gleans from historical research, his own life and upbringing, and the incredible actors around him to create a performance both unforgettable and continuously evolving.

I think this book is required reading for any actor halfway serious about their craft: it will remind you how many tools you have at your disposal; how imagination, empathy and discipline can coalesce to transport you as an actor, and in turn us, as the audience.

I am so grateful Giles took notes on his process and turned them into the book you're holding. I was already in awe of his performance; now I'm in awe of his humanity and attention to detail, and willingness to share the hard work and magic that goes into it: thanks for letting us into the room. The world is wide enough for us all, indeed.

Siempre,
Lin-Manuel Miranda

INTRODUCTION

When I was thirteen years old, my mother took my sisters and me on our one and only family holiday. Though she herself was from Barbados, she took us to Africa. Having never been abroad, I was both nervous and excited.

The trip would last a month and a half, which meant we'd miss a couple of weeks of school, so, before we left, Mum handed me a notepad and suggested I keep a journal of the experience. I asked what I should write and she told me, 'Write down what you see and hear—and what it *feels* like.' So I did.

That's how I came to start writing journals. Whenever I would set out on a journey I would keep a diary, write notes, scribble observations. Later, when I became an actor, I found this exercise useful in rehearsal. It pushed me to sharpen my senses. To be specific about what I was experiencing. To pay attention to the details of what I was seeing and hearing and feeling. It became a part of my working process.

15

And that's how I came to keep a journal when I got the role of Aaron Burr in Lin-Manuel Miranda's musical *Hamilton* in the West End. I took notes as I researched the part, as we rehearsed the show, and finally as we performed it at the Victoria Palace Theatre. The difference with this being *Hamilton*, though, was that the intensity of the situation was like nothing I'd experienced before. Therefore I had to write my notes whenever and wherever I could. In the rehearsal room. On trains. Always standing up. Mostly I wrote in my journal, but if that wasn't to hand I'd scribble thoughts, observations and questions on scraps of paper or even in the back cover of whatever Burr biography I happened to be reading that week.

A year after I'd left the show I came across the journal and found myself reading it. It was interesting to look at it from a distance. To be reminded how hard we worked, how much fun we had, how much I learned, and how much my thoughts and feelings about the character and story changed during the year I played the part. It struck me as the kind of thing I'd liked to have read when I was starting out as an actor. So I decided to use the journal to write this book, in the hope that a journey which was so special to me might perhaps be of use to others.

Because the journal wasn't written to be published—essentially a hurried collection of observations and impressions—I have tidied it up in places, though I have left what I call the 'funky syntax', the odd unfinished line and some of the lists I wrote during rehearsals, as these are results of writing in the furnace of the experience. They remind me of what it felt like being in the rooms where it all happened.

But, dear reader, remember that this is, of course, only my perspective. Each member of our company had their own journey through *Hamilton*, and the show means something different to each of us. Just as it has a different meaning to everyone who sees and hears it.

I am often asked to explain why. Why *Hamilton* is so extraordinary. What's the secret? It is neither my intention nor my task to answer that in this book. What I do know, however, is that in the very first line of the show Aaron Burr asks:

> How does a bastard, orphan, son of a whore and a
> Scotsman, dropped in the middle of a forgotten
> Spot in the Caribbean by providence, impoverished,
>   in squalor,
> Grow up to be a hero and a scholar?

He does not ask '*Why* does a bastard, orphan . . . ?' He specifically uses the word '*How?*' Very different.

My intention in this book is not to explain the Why of *Hamilton*, but to try and show you the How.

Your obedient servant,
G.T.

DRAMATIS PERSONAE

This is the original cast and creative team for the London production of *Hamilton*, many of whom feature throughout the book.

Ensemble	**Jade Albertsen**
Peggy Schuyler/ Maria Reynolds	**Christine Allado**
George Eacker/ Ensemble	**Curtis Angus**
Ensemble	**Johnny Bishop**
Ensemble	**Courtney-Mae Briggs**
Samuel Seabury/ Ensemble	**Jack Butterworth**
Hercules Mulligan/ James Madison	**Tarinn Callender**
Swing	**Jon-Scott Clark**
Ensemble	**Kelly Downing**
Charles Lee/Ensemble	**Leslie Garcia Bowman**
Swing	**Lia Given**
Eliza Hamilton	**Rachelle Ann Go**
Swing/Dance Captain	**Gregory Haney**
Ensemble	**Leah Hill**
Swing	**Barney Hudson**

Alternate Alexander Hamilton/Standby	**Ash Hunter**
Philip Schuyler/ James Reynolds/ Doctor/Ensemble	**Waylon Jacobs**
King George	**Michael Jibson**
Angelica Schuyler	**Rachel John**
Standby	**Aaron Lee Lambert**
Ensemble	**Miriam-Teak Lee**
Swing	**Phoebe Liberty**
Standby	**Sifiso Mazibuko**
Ensemble	**Gabriel Mokake**
Marquis de Lafayette/ Thomas Jefferson	**Jason Pennycooke**
Swing/Assistant Dance Captain	**Alexzandra Sarmiento**
John Laurens/ Philip Hamilton	**Cleve September**
Standby	**Marsha Songcome**
Swing	**Christopher Tendai**
Aaron Burr	**Giles Terera**
Swing	**Lindsey Tierney**
George Washington	**Obioma Ugoala**
Alexander Hamilton	**Jamael Westman**

Jeffrey Seller   Sander Jacobs   Jill Furman
The Public Theater
and
Cameron Mackintosh
present

HAMILTON

Book, Music and Lyrics by
Lin-Manuel Miranda

Inspired by the book *Alexander Hamilton* by
Ron Chernow

Scenic Design	**David Korins**
Costume Design	**Paul Tazewell**
Lighting Design	**Howell Binkley**
Sound Design	**Nevin Steinberg**
Hair and Wig Design	**Charles G. LaPointe**
Associate Choreographer	**Stephanie Klemons**
Musical Director	**Richard Beadle**
Musical Arrangements	**Alex Lacamoire** and **Lin-Manuel Miranda**
Music Supervision and Orchestrations by	**Alex Lacamoire**
Choreography by	**Andy Blankenbuehler**
Directed by	**Thomas Kail**

A NOTE ON THE
REHEARSAL PROCESS

A musical will generally rehearse for between four and six weeks in a rehearsal studio. The company will learn and rehearse the whole show with the director, choreographer, musical director, usually working with just a piano rather than the whole orchestra.

Following this initial period, the company moves into the theatre for the technical rehearsal—or 'tech'—where the cast is joined by the rest of the technical team—lighting, sound and costume designers—and the entire company methodically works through the show on the newly constructed set, scene by scene, song by song, adding, adjusting and fixing all the lights, sound, set, costumes and props in the production. The tech for a big musical production can last two weeks, as there is so much to be done during that time.

The orchestra will have been rehearsing separately while work is taking place at the theatre, but at some point during the tech, the orchestra and cast will meet for the first time to play and sing through the score together at a special rehearsal called the sitzprobe.

Once the tech has been completed—with the whole production rehearsed on stage with all its elements in place—the show goes in front of a paying audience for the preview performances.

During previews, which can last up to four weeks, the cast and creative team are still working on the show during the daytime. Lighting is still being honed; elements of costume, choreography, scenes and even songs might be adjusted, replaced or even cut. The production works this way throughout previews up until the opening night, when the show is finally ready and presented to the press for reviews (hence it sometimes being referred to as 'press night').

The West End production of *Hamilton* followed this order of events.

HAMILTON
AND ME

PART ONE

AUDITION

y. ~~[crossed out]~~. london bright, cold o

e City of london Cemetery where my mother

burried. Spend time with them. Rows of

blue sky. Came back to scho. Gym. Run

stretch. Warm up. Hamilton final at 5.

e to be at Camerons. They change it half

day. 40? Forty is supposed to be grow

. Responsible. Settled. I feel none of

My father was dead at 34. I never a

t. Voice feels ok at the gym. The tru

e. lin Manuel will be there later. h

much. Much water. Time to go.

get there to early and see or hear all

better suited to the part, yet most

of time. Walk. Waterloo. Southwark.

ich~ ill answer the phone. I'll eat a

dy after. People walking back to the Wa

heading in. Start to get doll

the room. Thats lin Manuel.

WEDNESDAY 14 DECEMBER 2016

Today it's my fortieth birthday and I was offered the role of Aaron Burr in *Hamilton*.

I woke early. London—bright, cold, clear. I go to the City of London Cemetery where my mother and father are buried. Spend time with them. Rows of gravestones and blue sky. I come back home to Soho. Gym. Run. Thirty mins. Stretch. Warm up. *Hamilton* final audition is at 5 p.m. Southwark. It was due to be at the Cameron Mackintosh offices in Bloomsbury. They switch it halfway through the day to the main audition rooms in Southwark.

Forty? Forty is supposed to be grown up. Respectable. Responsible. Settled. I feel none of these things. My father was dead at thirty-four. I never anticipated passing that.

Voice feels okay at the gym. The treadmill doesn't lie. Lin-Manuel will be there later. Haven't met him yet. Wonder what he'll be like? Don't think about it. What to eat? Not much. Much water. Time to go. Don't want to be there too early and see or hear all the other gentlemen better suited to the part than me, yet I must be there in good time. Walk. Waterloo. Southwark. Still sun. Just. Birthday almost gone. After the audition I'll answer the phone. I'll eat after. Think about birthday after.

People walking back to Waterloo Station from work. Me heading in. Nearly dark. Walk in the room. That's Lin-Manuel. There's Tommy. Alex. It's good to see them again. Cameron. Apart from to identify each face, my mind is concentrated on one thing only: Aaron Burr. All the preparing. Learning. Working. Researching. Trying. Singing. All of that serves to get you to this point. Yes. But now. Now it's time to let go.

An hour later I'm walking back across Waterloo Bridge. Stars. The river moves silently. How do I feel? Lighter. The bright, blurry London night is a beautiful place to walk alone. Dinner with Mark in Holborn. Phone rings as soon as we sit down. My agent, Simon: 'We'll have an offer first thing in the morning. Happy birthday.'

Rewind.

Six months prior to that night I was rehearsing a tour with Shakespeare's Globe Theatre. *Merchant of Venice*. I was playing the Prince of Morocco. Jonathan Pryce playing Shylock. We were starting in Liverpool. The week before we were to travel up there, my agent had messaged me and said, 'You should listen to this new show that everyone's talking about in New York. *Hamilton*.'

Oddly enough, the previous night, a friend of mine had texted me from New York saying, 'I've just seen the greatest show I've ever seen in my life. *Hamilton*. You have to be in it.' The proximity of these two messages unnerved me. I hadn't heard the show, but I'd heard *of* it. Wasn't it hip hop? They'll want someone hip hop. Not me. Was the excuse I shot back. But I could tell it was an excuse. Covering up for what? I knew nothing about the piece. Sometimes bells just ring. And when they do they can scare. 'You should listen to it,' Simon said.

'Cameron's bringing it over next year. They want to see you for it.'
'Which part?' I said.
'Aaron Burr.'
'Who's Aaron Burr?'

It takes me two hesitant days to go and buy the cast recording. Something told me to listen to it from my own hands rather than YouTube. Plus it gave me a chance to stall.

The same day I go and buy the CD I bump into a friend of mine in Covent Garden. 'Are you going to be in *Hamilton*? You have to play that part, the narrator.' I didn't tell her I had the album in my bag.

I go home. '*HAMILTON. AN AMERICAN MUSICAL.*' Double CD. I unwrap it and put it in the player. My finger pauses over the play button. What's wrong with me? What is this? PLAY.

Halfway through the first song it's clear I am in the presence of something extraordinary, and by halfway through the second song I know that I know this man, Aaron Burr. Somehow. Like I know myself.

When I get to the end of the album I go back to the beginning and listen to the whole thing again. Again, when I get to the end, it makes me cry. I text my agent: 'This is the greatest thing I've ever heard.' And I meant it. Lyric after lyric. Rhyme after rhyme. Melody after stunning melody. Such moving wit. Such intelligence. All in the service of a breathtaking story. And this man. 'I think I have to play this part.' That certainty is what terrifies. That is what makes us want to run and hide. It's rare, maybe once or twice in your life, when you just feel something. Something which can't immediately be explained. A bell just rings. A clarity occurs and the thing is there in front of you.

Achieving . . . ah, now that's the hard part. What to do? Acknowledge the bell. Then roll your sleeves up and work like a bastard.

Simon said, 'Well, good, because Cameron's bringing it over and they want to see you for it. You're going to be away on tour when they audition so I've set something up for New York for when you're out there. Start learning those songs.'

So I get to work. Every second I can find, I am learning this material. Going over and going over and going over. Never was I so happy as when, on my morning run round Liverpool's Albert Dock, I was able to get through the first verse of 'The Room Where It Happens'.

That was the start of July. Two weeks later we are performing *Merchant of Venice* at Lincoln Center in New York.

I hadn't told anyone I was auditioning, but a few days before we arrived in America I got found out. Jolyon, a friend in the *Merchant* cast, caught me practising 'Dear Theodosia' in the corridor on a tea break from rehearsals. Busted. So I had to confess. 'You're fucking shitting me!' I told him I was auditioning and they were letting me see the show when we were in NY and I had another ticket if he wanted to come.

The morning we arrive in Manhattan I head out for a run round Central Park. Jolyon is trying to give up smoking so says he'll come along. I suggest a little route: up as far as the reservoir and then back down the east side to the zoo. Fine. We make it up to the reservoir and start coming down. The sun is blazing even at 10 a.m. and after a while we're both pouring sweat. So I tell him we can stop. 'Nah, not yet. I'm fine. Keep going.' But after another five minutes I start to worry for him.

'Fuck you.' He gasps. 'Let's keep going. No pain, no gain.'

Five minutes later he finally says, 'Okay. That's good. I'm done when you are.'
I say, 'Okay, why don't we go as far as that statue over there?'

Two or three hundred yards later we gasp our way to a standstill by the large white statue we'd seen on the grass. He leans against it, looks up and says, 'Look!' The plinth simply reads 'HAMILTON'. We look up and there he is, looking down at us. One hand on his chest and the other holding papers.

Two days later we watched the show. I think Lin and Leslie Odom Jr. had only just left the show. I had been swimming in this piece for three weeks straight, but nothing prepared me for actually seeing it. We sort of staggered out onto the sidewalk at the intermission. The July sun just setting, and I remember thinking, what am I seeing?

Next day, after rehearsals and before the show, I jump in a cab, head downtown and meet Alex Lacamoire. *Hamilton*'s musical director. I'm a little scared, but I needn't have been—he is amazing and generous and open and funny and encouraging. I sing the material I'd spent the last few weeks trying to learn during *Merchant* rehearsals. It seems to go well. We have fun. So much so that we run over and now I'm late. I have to be back at Lincoln Center in ten minutes for *Merchant* performance number three.

I run back up Eighth Avenue. In rush hour. In the late-July dog-day afternoon heat. But I am happy. I got through the songs and didn't disgrace myself. Alex even said I did a good job. As I run up Eighth Avenue, sweating, I think to myself, if I look left down one of these streets—48th Street or 50th Street—I might just catch a glimpse of the trees of Weehawken across the river. But no time for that. The Prince of Morocco is waiting.

Next morning I wake up to a message from Simon: 'They liked you. They want you to go back today.'

So I did. Tommy Kail is there this time. Director. If I was scared to meet Alex, I'm even more scared to meet Tommy. I mean, whoever put this thing together must be a scary motherfucker. The fact that it's so packed with ideas, thoughts, journeys, yet each one delivered and realised with perfect clarity. That kind of storytelling ability doesn't stroll by every day. Whoever came up with this is going to have to be an intimidating presence.

As it happens, Tommy is cool. Equally as open and interested as Alex. He is slight. A mop of curly hair. Big smile. Watching eyes. A lean, coiled energy. He smiles and points at Alex: 'Well, *he* told me you were good, so let's go.' I do the same material. It didn't feel as settled as the day before, but I hadn't expected to have to come back. And the tag team of Aaron Burr and the Prince of Morocco had been kicking my ass all across the Atlantic. But Tommy seems happy. We talk. He's interested in who I am. Where I'm from. My parents. We part with a 'pleasure to meet you'.

The following week our tour moves to Washington, D.C. The 2016 Presidential Election is in full swing. Hillary or Trump? We make a trip to the White House. The Obamas are apparently in when we go. The building loaded with history. Being in that place proves a prodigious experience. I think of the building of a nation. And those upon whose backs it was built.

Then I hear nothing from *Hamilton* for a while. 'They said they'll see you at the finals in December. Keep on top of the material,' Simon says. I'm not so sure. 'They'll be getting the original cast over for London, surely? I wouldn't complain about that at all. They can have their pick. It's *Hamilton*.'

After D.C. our tour journeys to Chicago for two weeks. After that, China for a month and a half. Then back to the Globe for a month, and finally to Italy. Close in Venice. Nothing from *Hamilton*.

While we were in China I met up with a school friend of mine, Wai Wing. He and his wife showed me around Hong Kong on one of our afternoons off. I told him I'd been visiting the various temples of whichever city we were in, and he took me to one nearby. We lit incense and he explained to me different aspects of the many shrines there.

At the end of our visit, my friend sat me down in front of an old man who took the remaining incense sticks from my hand and squinted at them for a while, turning them over in his palm. He then told me, through Wai Wing's interpretation, that I had recently met someone of whom I should be wary, because although he was very brilliant and intelligent, he couldn't be trusted. I wasn't sure who he was talking about.

After the tour I arrive back in London. Dreaming about Aaron Burr. Seeing him in my mind's eye. Hearing him. So much of what people say to or about him in the show, people have said to me. I feel as if I know him. Like I know myself. This also strikes at the fear element. To peer at oneself is a very exposing thing. 'Stay on top of the material,' Simon keeps saying.

Autumn submits to winter. Still nothing from *Hamilton*. Simon: 'They'll see you at the final. Stay on top of it.' I do. I do what I know: work. I go to my mentor and singing teacher Nettie Battam down in Brixton. She's worked with everyone from Maria Callas to most of the musical theatre performers of the eighties and nineties. She gives me a funny look when I tell her it's a hip hop show, but when she makes me play her the music she claps, throws her head back and lets out a massive laugh: 'But, my darling, this is an opera.'

I find myself asking questions about this man. I began to read more about him. All I can find. Which is a lot less than the other Founding Fathers. The more I find, the more I want to know.

At the same time, part of me wants to resist getting too attached. What if? What if? If they'd wanted me they would have said something. Right? It's been four months. I hadn't wanted to tell anyone I'd auditioned. Not even my sisters. Why jinx it?

Then. The RSC call. *Titus Andronicus*. Would I come in for the role of Aaron the Moor? In all Shakespeare this is the one role where I thought I'd love to play that some day. And now is the first time in my life I feel as if I'd actually be able to. I go in and audition. They offer me the part. Aaron at the RSC.

Simon says, 'It clashes with *Hamilton*.'
'But we've heard nothing from them.'
'We have. They'll see you at the finals next month. I keep telling you.'

Aaron in Stratford or Aaron in Yorktown. In my waking hours there's no contest, of course, but once again the cool fear of getting one's hopes up for a part which feels in your DNA makes you flinch. What if? What if? Aaron offered or Aaron to reach for. Aaron to climb? Aaron to become?

'Can the RSC hold off for two weeks?'
'No. You have to make a decision now. Call me in the morning.'

I walk. Sit silently and I ask. Not to get the part—but for courage to hang on. Next morning I message Simon: 'Let's wait for it.'

That was mid-November. The final audition is December. December 14th. My birthday. Every day for those few weeks I get up and work. Sing. Read. Search. Try. Learn. Work. Sing. Read. Watch. Work. Wait.

And so, on December 14, Simon calls and says, 'We'll have an offer first thing in the morning. Happy birthday.'

I try to speak but no sound is coming out. He says, 'Don't speak. I'm going to hang up now before I start to cry. I'll speak to you in the morning . . . Aaron Burr.' The only words which form before hanging up: 'Thank you.'

Now, any actor will tell you that after you get a job first comes the fleeting moment of elation, then comes the panic. Holy shit. Now how do I do this? What do I really know about this man, Aaron Burr? That he befriends Hamilton and somehow ends up taking his life. What do I actually know about the American Revolution? It's too late to turn back now.

It was as if this person, this man who I'd been chasing all across the world, finally turned and said to me—Enough. Here's the deal, if you want to go on this journey you have to go all the way. Nothing less will do. Everything up till now has been a walk in the park. Now the real journey begins. And it will be like nothing you've ever known before. Some days will be brutal, others spectacular, but there's no backing out. There will be mountains and valleys. Dark nights and clear mornings. Pitfalls and snares. But remember—the higher the mountain, the sweeter the view. And if you truly want to go on this journey with me . . . then it's all the way.

PART TWO

REHEARSAL

...his being Hamilton it is encourage
...e introduce ourselves and what we
...l of sorts. If this done right each
...thing so that the whole thing sort
...really. Which is all anyone can hope
...filler makes a beautiful speech as
...this moment via experiencing the effect
..."A Broadway show which happened to
...cameras. Jeffrey has a very open face
...Measured and forward and full of
...to the way he speaks. And as y...
...and drawn in. Most impressive
...how far his heart is beating. '
...both apprehension and excitement.
...could be seen in negative and posi...
...his speech next. Funny. Everything
...in which all great makes seem to
...eyed person for the thing they do that

MONDAY 2 OCTOBER 2017

Jerwood Space.

Ten months I have been waiting for this day, and now it's here, I'm scared. That's okay. Mark texted saying, 'Relax and enjoy.' Tommy texted me last night: 'Have a good day tomorrow.' A good goal to have going into battle. I'll try.

I got in at 8.30 a.m. We start at 10. I have to warm up before rehearsal. I've spent a year listening, learning, reading, thinking, watching, researching, searching, marvelling, hoping, preparing. Now it's time to suck it up and do the thing. Equally excited and nervous. One thing I know from the past is that no matter how much you prepare and anticipate, nothing gears you for the experience. You find out by doing.

Alex Lacamoire calls the principals together in the downstairs music rehearsal room. Maestro. All smiles. All enthusiasm, patience and encouragement. These are not the things geniuses usually possess. Alex is a genius. No question.

It's beautiful to see everyone gathered. Fresh faces. Concentrated and ready. I can see that each has already been on her or his own unique journey to get to this point. Rachel John I know. Jason Pennycooke I've known forever. And Jamael Westman. Playing Hamilton. Right away we make each other laugh. He's tall. Rangy. Inquisitive. With a glint in his eye. I like him.

We are each given the score. A huge, A4-sized, very thick volume with sturdy plastic ring binders as a spine. I hold it in my hands. It has my name on the front and printed on each subsequent page as I let my thumb peel through it. The score is massive. Heavy. Hundreds of pages of staves, containing thousands of notes and bars and figures and letters and numbers. Each page to be deciphered and interpreted and understood. It occurs to me. It's a map. And each page will get us further up the mountain.

It's a funny feeling. A year ago this journey started out with two: me and Aaron Burr. Then Alex and Tommy joined—and the gang got a little bigger. Now, there are more of us. Everyone seems to fizz. The room is full of young, scrappy and hungry energy. This moment. I close my eyes and try to breathe this moment. It'll never be the first moment again. I try to look everyone in the eye. These are the eyes I'll be going up the mountain with. Each has heard their own bell, and each has answered it.

I try to remember what Tommy told me. We had breakfast a couple months ago when the creative team were over for more auditions. 'Don't feel pressure to recreate. Just create. You are here because of you.'

We talked that morning about lots. Not just the show. About everything. Childhoods. Shakespeare. China. Families. Life. What an extraordinary time it is for him. He's curious, full of stories, misses nothing. Jokes are his tools. Listens as much as he asks. Remembers things I'd forgotten I'd mentioned a year ago in New York. Information is important to him. He doesn't ask what he doesn't want to know. He seems, at the same time, open and mysterious. We click. Feels like I've known him since school. 'You are here because of you.'

Alex tells us we'll spend these first two weeks learning the score with him. Two-and-three-quarter hours of continuous music. Late next week, Tommy will arrive from NY, then the rest of the creative team, and then we'll have four more weeks to stage and rehearse after that. A long rehearsal period. We're working Saturdays. Americans love to work Saturdays. Boom. Let's go.

We are rehearsing at Jerwood Space, the biggest and I'd say best rehearsal studio in town. I like it. Southwark. You can walk by the river at lunchtimes. The production has taken four rehearsal rooms in the building. One where we can do break-out music calls, two downstairs where we can do scene work and dance sections, and the massive room at the top of the building in which is housed the vast set, including the revolves on which I'll try not to break my neck in the coming weeks. But that's the future. The only thing that matters here is now. This week is working through the score. Each song and every scene. Every note and every beat of the show.

By lunchtime my heart is full and my mind is wide-eyed.

But . . . we've started.

TUESDAY 3 OCTOBER

Wake in darkness. Gym. Stretch. Run. Warm up. What is my voice saying? Not sure yet.

Yesterday we were all in different rooms, learning and getting to grips with our songs. Each of us standing at the foot of our own mountain. Figuring out how we are going to reach the top and breathe the sweet air. There's a long way to get there.

My call today reads: '12 p.m. Mr Terera and Mr Lacamoire, Room 3, "Wait for It"/"The Room Where It Happens".'

Twin peaks. One—Macbeth; the other—Othello. The only thing to remember is: aim for fearlessness and take one step at a time. Lac had said he was looking forward to getting into rehearsals to see how we could make these songs my own.

When I first encountered the show, I immediately felt very connected to this part. I felt as if I knew this man very well. How he thought and moved and watched. As if I were staring into a mirror. Well, fine. That's one thing. Playing it is another matter. Sharing with an audience is a different matter still.

So at high noon I go to Rehearsal Room 3. Just Lac, the piano, and me and these songs. These moments. Situations. Words. We play and jam and Alex corrects me. Shows me. Stops me. Pushes me. Encourages me. Questions me.

The score is different from the cast recording. Rule number one that they tell you at drama school: never listen to a cast recording when preparing for an audition. Invariably it will be different in some way. Enough to throw you when you get into the room and the audition pianist plays what's on the score, not what you've been bopping round your bedroom to for the past week. Now, here, parts of what I've brought into the room are not what is in the score. Lac corrects me a couple of times before the penny drops. I freeze. A stark, lonely moment. A second of panic. My throat tightens. The guide rope falls away and I don't know what to do. But I don't stop. Come on, boy. The higher the mountain, the sweeter the view. There is only one thing *to do*. Learn afresh.

For months I have been focused on coming to this stage of the journey as prepared and full as possible. Books, books, more books. Films. Essays. More books. So. What do I do? Let it go. Discard all of it. Knowing that it is all in there somewhere. Whatever of my research that is of use will have been absorbed and available when I need it, but now I must start anew. It is a good thing. Let go of all that and begin afresh. Yes, this is what I must do. Be brave enough to wipe the page clean and start bare.

This is where I must start the show each night.

WEDNESDAY 4 OCTOBER

Jam, me, Cleve, Tarinn and Pennycooke are called for our Sons of Liberty tavern stuff and other bits we have together. Not with Lac, but with Richard Beadle, our musical director. He's young, scrappy . . . you know the deal. He's on it. He'd have to be to get picked by Lacamoire and Miranda.

The fellas sound amazing. A good start. It's so clear that the five of us have been in the company of these songs and words for a long time, but on our own. Now we actually get to say them *to* someone. To a Laurens who answers back. To a Mulligan who wants to impress. To a Lafayette who teases. We get to hear. Respond. Play. Interact. How he says *that* word informs how you say *this* word. How he throws out *that* line makes you throw *this* one back in return. Each of us relishing the shift in process from recital to contact sport.

Brothers immediately. We don't need to push it. It just seems to be there as we work.

Cleve and Tarinn bouncing off each other. Much laughter. Jase, more experienced, just lets them burn and fizz knowing that all he has to do is pick the right moment to throw in the shady one-liner that makes the room erupt. Me—quiet, and Jam—enjoying the banter but also seeing beyond it.

We sit with our scores on music stands in front of us and highlight our lines, record what we need to on our phones. Play. Take notes. Try stuff out. Trip. Laugh. Discard. Work our way through.

Next time through, I stand up. Sitting doesn't feel right now. The others follow. Off we go.

THURSDAY 5 OCTOBER

I woke up in the middle of the night and couldn't get back to sleep. I must have done, though, because I had that dream again. First one in a while. Actors' anxiety dreams usually come closer to getting in front of an audience. This wasn't quite that, though. It's reoccurring. Something that actually happened to me.

When I was a kid in the mid-eighties, there were two situations that would be on the news every day.

The Troubles in Northern Ireland and the troubles in South Africa. Both confused the hell out of me. You'd hear these words and I had no idea what they meant. Apartheid. Sinn Féin. Boycott. Protestant. Tear gas.

All I knew was that every day there'd be voices on the news saying that X number of people had been killed today. Both countries seemed to be at war, but had been invaded by no other nation. I knew that two sets of people were fighting in Ireland, and that in South Africa someone called Nelson Mandela was in prison. For some reason. I was thirteen. I couldn't remember a time when both these things were not present in my little life.

Well, my dream plays out what happened in real life. Almost.

One morning I'm up and playing on the carpet in front of the TV. The news comes on. A reporter with a microphone, making a report from Trafalgar Square. I find myself jumping up and running into the kitchen, saying to my mother, 'On the TV they're saying that they're going to make an announcement. They think they are going to release Nelson Mandela from prison.' I don't understand it all, but I know it's a big deal. Enough to run and tell her. My mother turns from the sink and says, 'Get dressed.'

An hour and a half later we walk into Trafalgar Square where the reporter had been standing. The

South African Embassy. A few hundred people are gathered in the street under its balcony. Stopping the traffic. The air is charged. Music plays. I'm a bit scared. The twenty-four-hour rolling anti-apartheid demonstration—which had been campaigning outside the embassy for freedom for the South African people and for Nelson Mandela, come rain or shine—is handing out flyers and placards. Some guys are playing drums. People are happy, though nothing has happened yet.

Then there's movement from the embassy balcony. Long net curtains are pulled aside, the doors open and two enormous conical speakers, which look like they haven't been dusted off since the end of the Second World War, are wheeled out, and a radio announcement crackles from them, announcing that the South African government is going to release Nelson Mandela after twenty-seven years in prison. The place erupts. Singing. Shouting. Dancing. Crying. Hugging. In the dream it is sunny, but in real life it was very cold. It was February. This is the only bit of the dream which differs from reality. My mother and I stay and dance and dance and dance with strangers and when we finally left she winked at me and said, 'See, life isn't just something you watch on TV. You are in it.'

★

The entire cast were together for the first time today to sing through the show. Principals, ensemble, swings. Now this is what I'm talking about. It was thrilling. Thirty of us. A lot of good energy. A mighty sound. Excitement.

SATURDAY 7 OCTOBER

Today by 6 p.m. my voice was in tatters. Singing from 10 to 6 every day is work. To vocalise notes is one thing. We place them in a certain place and sing. Rapping is not singing—but not quite speaking. It's heightened. Harder. If you're not used to it, that is. I'm trying to devise some warm-ups for myself to get myself used to it. But I guess I know that, as with all things, you get better by doing.

At the start you always have to dive in. Always. Throw yourself in. Let your body and your mind and your heart see what kind of world we are dealing with. Get to know the terrain. But you gotta lean into it or you'll slide.

The higher the mountain, the sweeter the view.

WEEK TWO

TUESDAY 10 OCTOBER

This morning we did 'Non-Stop', which ends the first half of the show. A lot of words. Jam wasn't there when I arrived. Katy Bryant, our company manager, made an announcement that Jam's partner had gone into labour so he is at the hospital. Beautiful news. Life. More life. I missed him today. What a year for him. What a time.

Earlier this year I did a play at the Donmar, then took a couple months off to prepare for this. I went to my sister's house out in the country while they were on holiday, and sat and learned the score. Each morning I got up and tried to tackle another song. Aaron is in almost all of them. I sat with the cat and studied and researched and fucked up and started again.

One thing I find useful as I'm learning a part is to get a notepad and write out each song from memory. Every word. The exercise tells me which bits I don't know. Which bits I've paraphrased. Generalised. It reveals where I am unsure. Ah, you thought you knew that sentence, but it's 'and' not 'but'. The little details which slip through the net of your mind are exposed and show clearly where you are not being specific. Also, it reveals certain things about the character's thinking process. Patterns. How often questions are asked. What he says of others. What others say of him. What are his favourite words? What imagery? This song is the one that trips me up most.

WEDNESDAY 11 OCTOBER

From the moment I open my eyes, I'm thinking about my voice. How is it today? Is it there? How clear? How tired? How responsive? How supple? Any performer knows this deal. From opera to panto. We are married to our voices—and care must be taken.

I remember two years ago bumping into a friend of mine in Covent Garden. He was just about to start rehearsals playing the lead in the original London cast of *Kinky Boots*.

'Okay, see you in a year's time then.' I grinned at him.
'Do you know what I mean!?' He smiled back.
'There's only one way to do it: eat well, get plenty of sleep and plenty of water. Say goodbye to your social life, and if you drink: don't.'

With this show, the physical commitment is one thing. That's a given. But the more we work, the more I see that it's the inner commitments which are in fact the more demanding.

What is it to point a gun at someone?
At someone you know.
At someone you care about.
What is it to kill someone?
In what state must someone be in order to murder?
What is murder?

An eighteenth-century duel was a very strange and particular thing. Two men arrange to meet, take aim at each other and fire, knowing that one or both may die. Knowing that you might walk away a murderer or not walk away at all.

Jam and I have talked about it. We've both read all the books and the essays. Tried to piece together for ourselves what took place that fateful morning. But, finally, what is it actually to stand and aim and fire? I feel that the answer to that lies in everything which comes before it. The strength of their bond when they first meet. The strength of the moments during 'A Winter's Ball' and the wedding. The strength of whatever it is that happens during their years as lawyers. As Hamilton says: 'Burr, my first friend.'

FRIDAY 13 OCTOBER

Today was the test. 'Dear Theodosia.' The most delicate song to sing. It's beautiful. It floats. Has in it all the promise of young men and young life.

Jam is still with his new family. A little girl. Almost certainly saying to her the very words Hamilton says to his newborn son Philip in the show: 'When you smile I am undone . . . Pride is not the word I'm looking for.'

After lunch we come to the song. It's not dreadful but it's not great. Lac is patient and encouraging, but I don't think I'm giving him what he wants.

Tommy arrived this morning. In the afternoon he walks in and everyone loses their shit. It's a beautiful moment.

'How's it going, buddy?'
'I'm not there yet.'
'Of course you're not. This is the end of Week Two. You're learning music and next week we'll move. You are allowed to not be there yet. You do know we have five weeks left, right? Gimme a break.'

SATURDAY 14 OCTOBER

Today we gathered to sing the whole show. To do this at the end of the week is tough, but it is an exciting way to end the week all the same.

The intention was always to have the official *Hamilton* 'meet and greet' today, now that the entire creative team is here, and afterwards sing the whole show from start to finish. Well, everyone except Lin, he's filming somewhere, I think. They say he'll be here in a few weeks.

The producers, including Jeffrey Seller and Cameron, and various people from departments are all here. Daunting, yes, but at least you know it's coming. Unavoidable. Fear has been a pretty present emotion for me thus far on this journey. My voice was a little tired by yesterday. Stands to reason. I'm putting it through a lot, so it's still trying to work out what the hell's going on. The big-blast requirements of 'Room Where It Happens' and 'Wait for It', the soft, subtle moments like 'Dear Theodosia' and 'The World Was Wide Enough', and the most difficult: the rap stuff. A grey sky as I walk into work—and as I walk, I resolve to simply try and take it one moment at a time.

We gather in the room, maybe seventy of us, and smile and try not to be nervous. Mingle. Grab a juice or a croissant. I take an apple.

Meet and greets at the start of rehearsals are almost unbearable at the best of times. It's always like the first day of school. Everyone terrified and paranoid, thinking everyone else is composed and calm. We stand in the obligatory circle—only, this being *Hamilton*, it is enormous—and one by one introduce ourselves and say what we do. It is a ritual of sorts and understood as such, it becomes both necessary and rather beautiful. If it's done right, enough people say something funny as they introduce themselves so that the whole thing serves as a form of icebreaker.

Jeffrey Seller makes a beautiful speech about his journey to this moment via experiencing the effect of witnessing his first Broadway show, which happened to be produced by Cameron. Jeffrey has a very open face and way of speaking. Measured and forward and full of enthusiasm. There is a joy to the way he speaks. And as you listen, you are moved and drawn in. Most impressively, though, he starts by saying how fast his heart is beating. This touches me. It at once suggests both apprehension *and* excitement. The balance of what could be seen as negative and positive. Cameron makes his speech next. Funny. Enthusiastic and with that same passion which all great makers seem to have. The same wide-eyed passion for the thing they do that they had on the first day they started doing it. That flame doesn't seem to diminish and, even though they may accomplish so much, it's still there, which makes it all the more affecting.

Then Tommy speaks. He often speaks of his interest in and use for the journeys which have brought a particular group of individuals together. All different stories and journeys, all propelled by different people or families, mentors, detractors. All pushing us towards this very moment when we are all stood together in a room to share something. This impresses me very much. I am utterly aware of all the hands which have steered me towards this moment. More so than anything I've ever done. Not only the people, but the work. The projects past. I am grateful to them and call on them now.

We break for lunch, then gather again to sing the entire show. Fewer people to watch now. Maybe twenty. The essential production team.

I speak the first words of the thing. The first word is 'How'. I'm reminded of *Hamlet*: its first word is 'Who'. I'm not entirely sure what's going to come out of my mouth when I go to sing. I suspect I'll start okay, but it's nearly three hours of music. Well, I finally say, I've done the work. I believe in that. I trust that. What must be achieved before anything happens is a sense of relaxation and playfulness. If my voice falters, it falters. We may not have another moment to stand and sing this whole show from start to finish, all of us, the entire company, again, so enjoy it. Use it. Try to find the freedom within it. That can only come through relaxation and clarity of intention. Don't try to do too many things at once. Just focus on what's in front of you.

Lac eyes me as everyone is settling down.
'Ready?'
'Mmm-hmm.' I nod.
The piano hammers out the first famous chords. I let the breath drop into my body and ask: 'How . . . '

Two-and-three-quarter hours later, all thirty of us sing the final line as one. No piano, just voices: 'Who lives, who dies, who tells your story?'

Silence. Then the room erupts in joy, relief, pride and excitement. We did it. Tommy and Lac seem happy. Our first collective victory.

Time to head home for a well-earned rest. But before we do, I huddle all of us actors together in the middle of the room. We put our arms around each other's shoulders and our heads touch. I find myself speaking.

'We'll probably never have this moment again, will we? From Monday we'll go upstairs. Moving, breaking off into different groups. We'll be split up more and more into principals and ensemble, swings and covers. All the bullshit labels. But the only thing that matters is that we are one company. One family. Things are about to step up a gear, but look what we achieved today. And we did it together. The only way we get through this is together. So let's look after each other, help each other, enjoy and encourage each other, and then we'll get where we wanna go.'

WEEK THREE

We move upstairs to the big rehearsal room. A mock-up of the entire stage set, including revolves, has been built and takes up the entire room. As with all rehearsal rooms, the floor is marked up with coloured tape. Different colours indicating the location of the front of the stage, any doors, stairs, entrances and exits into the wings.

The tape representing the front of the stage has numbers along it. In its centre is 0, then moving out from that, on both sides, is the number 2. Then 4. All the way out to the edge of the stage with 16. So 0 to 16 on the left- and right-hand sides of the stage. This way the whole stage can be seen as a grid, and moves and positions can be given and reproduced accurately.

Props are placed on head-height portable wooden shelves at the sides of the stage, in the position which in the theatre would be the wings. Some of the famous blue and cream army jackets have been brought over from the American costume department and are placed on hooks at the back of the room for us to rehearse in. I look in the inside pocket of the one I'm wearing. It says 'Christopher Jackson'.

We've been singing for two weeks solid. Eight hours a day. Now we stand. We move. We travel in the space—and search for answers.

Steph Klemons, our associate choreographer, has the entire show in her head. Every single character's moves and gestures. Her task is to go through each number and stage it, giving each actor their positions, traffic, choreography. Where you come on from, when you move, on what lyric, where you move to, who you pass, what prop you pick up, when you pick it up, who you give it to, where you exit. She has the track of every person in the cast in her head. The entire show. Thirty people. Fifty-odd songs. Two-and-three-quarter hours. You do the math.

'Okay, top of the show. I'm gonna need Burr. Burr, you come on from stage-right wing one. You come on from here and stand right here on 8, to say your first line. Okay? Okay, where's Laurens?' She moves off to Cleve and then Jason and then Tarinn, leaving me with my thoughts for a second.

Don't think about the mountain, think about the step.
I know where I stand, but why do I speak?
Why am I here?

Burr walks out to no music. In silence.
Walks on stage towards the audience.
Eyes them and speaks. 'How does a bastard . . . ?'
Why is he here? What is he here to do? What does
he want?

The first thing spoken is a question. I'm here for
answers.

If Steph is scary, Andy Blankenbuehler, our
choreographer, is intense, with a formidable artistic
focus. Like all good choreographers he was a dancer.
A great one. Everything he says comes from a deep-
felt sense of imagination. Every move, every gesture,
finger shift, he describes in emotional, imaginational
terms. He talks about what you as a person are
trying to do to someone else.

I watch as he and Steph construct the number
around me, beat by beat, step by step. The song
essentially charts Alexander's life from childhood in
the Caribbean to his arrival in New York. The first
twenty years of his life. And it does so in just under
four minutes. Not only do we get the hero's journey
so far, but the number also introduces all the main
characters in the story to the audience (except King
George). It's a masterclass in economy and
movement involving the whole company. Twenty
years. Four minutes. We spend the whole morning
on the number.

I'm glad that we are all involved. Less nerve-wracking to be all in it together. Of course, I forget my lyrics the moment I have to sing them while moving. I've been singing them for a year and a half every day and *now* they go. That's okay. I look around the room and it's happening to all of us. We've been sat singing for two weeks, but now we have to bring on that chair, place that table, carry that rope, pass that book, that letter. We have to see the ship setting sail, have to attach those ropes, move those sacks, have to spin past that sailor, we have to turn and see . . . Alexander Hamilton. There he is, disembarking the ship with his bag, arriving and stepping onto American soil.

The first time we run it all together, after many minutes of explaining and showing and teaching, somehow it works. There's a lot of almost bumping into each other and being in the way of tables and arms, and it seems like almost all of what Lac taught us in the last fortnight evaporated, but no one gets concussion and somehow we get to the end of the number. Now what we have to do is work. Practise. Repeat. Go again. Get better. Improve. We take notes. Write. Work. Write. Work.

TUESDAY 17 OCTOBER

Buy Jason a gift!

[Jason Pennycooke got hold of my journal and left me a message while I was rehearsing 'Aaron Burr, Sir'.]

A month or so before we started rehearsal, Jam and I discussed the idea of a trip to America. The Weehawken duelling-ground site essentially still exists across the river from Manhattan.

'Fuck it, let's do it. I'm down,' Jam said. But in the end we couldn't quite make the timing work. It would have been interesting, of course, but now that we are in the reality of rehearsals, with actual bodies, minds and interactions, I'm reminded that the most important places for an actor to visit are the ones inside his or her own soul. The duelling grounds within.

So.

As Burr and Alexander first meet outside the tavern, Burr doesn't want to stop. What am I in the middle of doing? I'm reading a book. What book? Then this kid steps up, but I'm busy. Then something within the conversation stops me. And suddenly my focus is completely on him. This moment is everything.

The things which make a story or a character compelling are the 'What if . . . ?' moments. What if Alexander hadn't approached Aaron that day? What if I hadn't stopped? But I do. Why?

While Steph is teaching everyone else their tracks, and while Cleve, Jase and Tarinn practise their shit, Jam and I grab a moment to play.

Something within the conversation changes Burr. Hamilton starts by talking a lot, blurting out information that I didn't ask for. Compliments and flattery. My replies are short. Give nothing away. I answer his first question with a question. Classic Burr.

– Pardon me. Are you Aaron Burr, sir?
– That depends. Who's asking?

I suspect, even at this young age, Burr is used to people knowing who he is and treating him differently. He comes from a high family. Laurens is about to refer to him as the prodigy of Princeton college.

There is certainly something about this scrappy, hungry kid's persistent enthusiasm—'How'd you graduate so fast?'—but not enough to keep me from dismissing him with a defusing sarcasm. But then, all of a sudden, I shift. I cut him off in fact. 'Can I buy you a drink?'

This is the start of their story. This is the moment everything is set in motion. There is a direct line from this moment right through to Weehawken. I notice a twin sentence right at the other end of their journey at the end of the play. During 'The World Was Wide Enough', the first thing Burr does after having shot Alex: 'I get a drink.' Everything that has happened between those two drinks. Does he go back to that same tavern? To drink that same drink?

'Can I buy you a drink?' What makes me change and say this? I find always that the answer to my questions in rehearsals can be pinpointed directly and precisely in what has just been said. Obvious, I know, but as actors we get caught up in our own shit. The answers always lie not in what you say but what you hear.

What happens, of course, is Hamilton's discovery that Aaron Burr is also an orphan:

– You're an orphan?
  Of course! I'm an orphan.
  God, I wish there was a war!
  Then we could prove that we're worth more than anyone bargained for . . .
– Can I buy you a drink?

The information about their origins is one thing, but the fascinating thing is what Hamilton does with that information. Jam and I play, and I notice something. The instant Hamilton learns that they are both orphans, his whole attack on Burr changes and he immediately treats him differently.

I go and look on the page and notice something. Everything from Hamilton up until that moment has been 'I'—'I, I, I'—'Me, Me, Me'. I count. In the short conversation so far, he has said the word 'I' or 'I'm' thirteen times. The moment Hamilton finds out that they are both orphans—'You're an orphan? Of course! I'm an orphan.'—he, for the first time, uses the word 'We': 'God, I wish there was a war! Then we could prove that we're worth more than anyone bargained for . . . '

It happens just like that. It's immediate. Before that moment it's 'I', and after that moment it's 'We'.

Suddenly, for the first time in their encounter, Burr is not dealing with some flattering kid who is using all his energy trying to put him on a pedestal— rather, he is suddenly in the presence of someone who considers them both equals. On a fundamental level.

I suspect Burr is used to people thinking of him as different: 'The prodigy of Princeton college' . . . 'Burr, you disgust me' . . . 'You are the worst, Burr' . . . What if he's used to people saying 'You' and suddenly here is someone saying 'We'?

Hamilton digests this information and shifts, and, as a result, Burr finds himself shifting too. 'Can I buy you a drink?'

Of course, Burr isn't standing there counting how many times Hamilton uses the word 'I'. That's not how we, as humans, work. Life happens too quick for that. What happens is that we're going along, we meet someone and somehow, on some level, for some reason, we just click. Suddenly you are just chatting over a drink. Just like that you are friends. It happens and you don't question it. You go with it.

For both these young men, this day was supposed to go differently. But for whatever reason, fate steps in.

WEDNESDAY 18 OCTOBER

'The Schuyler Sisters.'

In the afternoon, Tommy pulls me aside to go through my stuff. He directs by stealth. Prompting, questioning, guiding, steering. Unlike a lot of directors he knows when to use words and when he doesn't need to. I've only ever met one other director who was also able to, at times, direct you without saying a word and that's Peter Brook.

We talk American history.

One of the things it's been fascinating for me to learn is the diverse nature of the American colonies. One thinks of the Revolutionary War as King George's Britain against a colonialist, God-fearing, Puritan monolith. Ron Chernow, however, in the book which inspired this show, details a collage. Thirteen colonies of different beliefs, faiths, languages even. The common cause was freedom from Britain, but among themselves they fought, bickered and seemed always on the brink of destroying one another. The Founding Brothers' task was to unite to get rid of George and then *stay* united to try and realise the very thing they were fighting for. The first half of our play deals with the former, the second half the latter. One of the many brilliant things about this production is how it tells the story of that diversity through its casting choices.

Tommy tells the story of a diverse group coming together to create something which is greater than the sum of them by creating a diverse group who come together to create something which is greater than the sum of them.

Ours is a troupe made up of all sorts of folk. Everyone from different backgrounds and beliefs and places, with one thing in common: the work. 'We rise and we fall, and we break, and we make our mistakes.'

There's Rachel John. She's playing Hamilton's sister-in-law Angelica Schuyler. A proper East London girl. Her parents from Trinidad. I call her 'Our Sister Beloved'. The life and soul of the family. Funny, feisty, real and caring. She and Tommy have a great double act when they get to teasing. If one of us is feeling low, she'll pick us back up.

Cleve September—playing John Laurens and Hamilton's son Philip. Born and raised in South Africa. Hungry, eager to get it right.

Jason Pennycooke—playing Lafayette and Thomas Jefferson (Laf/Jeff). Some of his people were from

Nevis like Hamilton. We tease him cos he's the oldest. He's been in every show you can think of. I first worked with him years ago on *Rent*. He played Benny. I sort of hero-worshipped him. He's the real deal.

Leslie Garcia Bowman—William P. Van Ness. From New Zealand. His mother is from the Philippines. A couple years ago he got himself a place at a drama school here in London and so tap danced on street corners in New Zealand to raise money to get himself here. He's that one guy in a group that *everyone* likes.

Leah Hill—she plays the Bullet in the fatal duel. Tiny but mighty. She don't take no shit.

Rachelle Ann Go (Shin)—Hamilton's wife Eliza. From the Philippines. Always has a smile of encouragement. We met at our final audition. Hugged to calm each other—and from that moment we were brother and sister.

Michael Jibson—King George. From Hull, I think. Good Northern lad. Gets teased because we never see him. He comes to rehearsal to do his number and then fucks off and we won't see him for a week when he gets to do his next.

Obioma Ugoala (Obi)—George Washington. Towering. Half-Nigerian, half-Irish. Seems older than his years. Politically minded. Opinionated. Ah, but underneath . . .

Kelly Downing. From Coventry. Good energy. I like her. Always seems happy. If you're furious, just look around—she'll be smiling.

Christine Allado—Maria Reynolds and Peggy. Born in the Philippines. Like Shin, she's an actual legit star. Sings all over the world with incredible people.

Jack Butterworth—Samuel Seabury. From Liverpool. The best dancers dance as if they have a secret. Jack's one of those.

Tarinn Callender—Hercules Mulligan and James Madison. His people are from Barbados, like mine. Sturdy. Hench. Again, older than his years. Life and soul. He's like that uncle who'll do anything to get a laugh.

Johnny Bishop, our pocket-sized Trinidadian. He always seems to be warming up in a corner somewhere. He always wears a shirt in rehearsals. As in button-up with a collar. Like a full-on cotton shirt. I get through at least two T-shirts a day. There's very little time to stand and really see people work, but whenever I see him dance I am awestruck.

And then there's Jam. Tall. Irish Jamaican London. Fresh out of RADA. Fierce intellect. Seemingly as calm and relaxed as the day is long. He has this extraordinary quality. He's part-monk, part-pirate, but for the most part he's monk. Calm. Centred. Disciplined. Concentrated. Watchful. And then, all of a sudden, the pirate will show up. Mischievous.

Anarchic. Rebellious. Libertine. Impulsive. Almost destructive. He's the smartest person in the room. Hands down. His mind capable of working in multiple directions at once. Perfect for Hamilton. We talk a lot. But when we're working on our feet little needs to be said. I feel like sometimes I know what he's going to do before he does it. Sometimes I sense vice versa. I hope we can keep that when we get to the theatre.

I could go on. Between us, our parents must represent over a dozen countries. It moves me to think of all the struggles they endured, sacrifices they made, journeys they took, in order for us all to be in this room now.

'We'll give the world to you, and you'll blow us all away . . .'

THURSDAY 19 OCTOBER

'Right Hand Man.'

Watching Andy choreograph—or, more accurately, reveal his choreography—is a prodigious and unforgettable thing. I have met few people who can express movement, both the movement of the body and the movement of the space, so forcefully as him. His passion is total. His countenance intense. Super-intense. As choreographers often are. Considering they have to envisage multiple moving parts at the same time, I am always surprised at their singular focus. With Andy it is at once intimidating and awe-inspiring.

After lunch, Jam and I find ourselves having a conversation. The nature of Alexander and Aaron's relationship. Their paths. Both of us are trying to square the historical record with the story on the page in front of us. There is a time for research and then a time for imagination. Ultimately, all that is important is what's on the page.

But here's the thing. What I love about Lin's play are the gaps in between the songs.

What happens between the scene in Washington's office during 'Right Hand Man', when Burr gets bumped for Alexander, and when they next see each other in 'A Winter's Ball'? What has happened for me? What happens between their moment leading into 'Wait for It' and the next time they meet after the war? What happens between 'Non-Stop' and 'The Room Where It Happens'? Significant things. Dig in the words deep enough and we find out.

FRIDAY 20 OCTOBER

'Right Hand Man' Continued.

Summer falls away to autumn. Bringing with it the dark days.

The cast have had so much information thrown at us that people move about the rehearsal room looking more than a little dazed. When people, groups, are thrust together for intense periods of time—whether it's on a ship or the *Big Brother* house—a bonding starts to occur.

Time starts to bend and warp. The ordeal that is being experienced can only be truly appreciated by your fellow victims. Even Tommy, Lac, Andy and Steph's experience and perspective will be different to ours. The cast are bearing up, but we are approaching the moment when there will be tears.

Before then, though, comes the hysteria. Which is the stage we're at now. A sort of survival mode kicks in. All the information and anxiety tricks the nervous system into thinking the body is in danger of its life. The long hours. The repetition. A kind of wired, frenetic verve takes over the body and mind. It is at once exhausting and exhilarating. It helps you keep going.

Going in to the wedding scene, Jam and I talk camaraderie. More fun. We tease and wind each other up now.

SATURDAY 21 OCTOBER

[Some lists and notes I made.]

ALEXANDER/AARON

Same height—5'6"
Same weight.

Same age. 1756.
No father. No father.
Clothes important.

Jefferson—14 years older.

A.B.—Amulet of Mary Wollstonecraft wore all his life
A.H.—Never received an electoral vote for president
A.B.—Intimate friends with Native Americans
A.B.—Received Blacks to dinner

Dolly Madison selected A.B. as guardian of her son and trustee of estate.
Abigail Adams—wrote John Adams—she prefer A.B. to succeed him. Over Jefferson.

THINGS SAID ABOUT A.B.

LAURENS—Prodigy of Princeton college

ANGELICA—You disgust me

LAFAYETTE—You are the worst, Burr

ALEXANDER—I will never understand you
You stand only for yourself
Amoral
Dangerous
Disgrace
Always considered you friend
Jefferson has beliefs, Burr has none
No one knows what you believe

My first friend
My enemy

MADISON—Attractive in the north
Obfuscates
Dances
A less extreme you (Jeff)

JEFFERSON—Not forthcoming

PUBLIC—Approachable

MUSIC
Nina Simone—'Feelings'. Montreux
Mozart Requiem—Introit and Kyrie
'Dinner at Eight'—Wainwright
Tosca—Tito Gobbi/Callas—'Vissi d'arte'
'Walk Idiot Walk'—The Hives

SUNDAY 22 OCTOBER

The Legend of President Burr.

I discovered something. There's a book written by one of Burr's contemporaries. As often happened in the eighteenth and nineteenth centuries, when people of note died, their papers were given to some associate who collated a kind of memoir of that person. A posthumous autobiography of sorts.

I found Burr's. Long out of print and I've never seen it referred to in other books. But there it was, buried in the dusty far reaches of the internet.

These types of books basically take the form of an official timeline of the person's life. No dirt, but anything contemporaneous is useful. In the book, I suddenly notice something.

Whoever wrote the book knew Burr as a young man. The writer details the well-known facts about Burr's family. All theologians. All mighty 'fire and brimstone' preachers. He also notes the other much-spoken fact that Burr's father, Reverend Aaron Burr Sr, was founder of Princeton University. But, whenever this writer, this contemporary of Burr's, refers to Burr Sr he calls him 'President Burr'. Not 'Aaron Burr Senior' or 'Burr's father'. *President* Burr. Aaron Sr, as well as being founder, was indeed also President of the university, and it appears that during and after his life he was known by one and all in New York as President Burr. Aaron never knew his father, but would presumably have spent his childhood, youth, formative years and adulthood hearing the legends of President Burr:

'You're President Burr's boy . . . '
'I knew President Burr . . . '
'The night President Burr addressed the hall . . . '

The Presidential Election of 1800 which leads to the duel was about more than politics then.

WEEK FOUR

MONDAY 23 OCTOBER

I came close today. Tears. Only taken three weeks. I've never had that before. Ever. Partly because or mainly because I feel out of control. Or not in control of my process.

The sheer volume of information being thrown at us is massive and multilayered. This in itself is not unexpected or unwanted. Information is what I crave, expect and welcome. The issue is how to collate and ingest the info I need. Choreography, steps, positions, cues to move, cues to arrive, cues to stop, which steps go with which lyrics. My life is bits of paper with instructions scrawled in pencil.

I'm good at remembering things once I've been told. Any move I make I have to fix to whatever my intention is at the time, so it's easy to remember once you have that connection, but that's not the point. The point is I'm on stage for virtually the whole show, therefore in pretty much every scene that gets rehearsed. I'm struggling to find the time during the day to go over, collate and implement what we've done.

Burr walks on stage at the top of the show, followed by the whole company, and pretty much everyone is dancing, singing, acting during every song (well, practically—see George III!). Therefore there's two-and-three-quarter hours' worth of music and choreography to learn. I'm finding it hard to process and practise.

Steph will often give everyone their moves, steps, positions, all the lifts and jumps and combinations, ten or fifteen minutes of complicated instructions. Then to me: 'Oh yes, Burr. You walk from here to here when she says "Alexander". Okay?' Which sounds simple enough—a child could do it: the character walks from here to here—but inevitably, because it's such a seemingly easy bit of staging, I won't get to go through it with the company. Who are loudly, hurriedly going through the choreography they've just been given.

Steph claps. 'Okay! We're going to go from "Raise a glass".' Cool. I have my cue to move. I know where I'm moving to. We start. As does the revolve. Wait a minute. No one mentioned the revolve moving. My cue coming up. Horror. Just as I am about to step, two actors are now standing right in front of me. Another is coming this way. Legs and arms whirl past. Do I go first? Do they go first? Who has right of way here? I haven't even stepped on stage yet. Oh shit. My cue has come up. Actor Rule Number One: whatever else is happening, when your cue comes up, crack on.

So. I step. Car crash. Horse-drawn carriage crash. Then, in the space where I was supposed to be walking, is a couple doing a beautiful lift, while the inner turntable is moving. Bodies, moving stages, traffic. Wagon crash. Me, attempting not to scatter everyone like bowling pins. Failing. Flailing. I look up and catch Steph's eye, who, though trying to survey a stage full of expertly delivered choreography, cannot help but be drawn to the chaos being wrought by Burr as he flaps his way through the scene like a seasick goose. Once we stop I get given the inevitable note about my bit. Which was by far the simplest task anyone just had to execute.

'Um, Burr, what was going on over there?'

I'll have completely understood what I *ought* to have done, but—and here's the rub—I won't have had the opportunity to practise it with the elements involved. Bodies. Sets. Revolves. Props. I never get that. Frustrating. Well. Keep going, boy.

The higher the mountain . . .

TUESDAY 24 OCTOBER

I worked like a bastard between . . . well, overnight. The idea of falling behind does not appeal. The only option is work. Work, work and further work. I am getting closer. 'The Schuyler Sisters', 'Helpless', 'Satisfied' all contain a lot of movement for me. That which I could not do yesterday I can at least attempt today. Subsequently I felt less dejected today. Also, one has to keep a sense of perspective. Unless there is joy in the work, it cannot be all it can be.

Just before lunch, Andy gave a brilliantly helpful insight into the character of Burr within the staging of the show. One thing he said in particular: 'With the character of Hamilton, everything is staged in circles. The turntable. Everything is circular and spinning. A hurricane. With Burr, everything is square. Four-sided. Boxed in. Until he has no choice but to be staring down the barrel of a pistol at Alexander.'

I had been aware of the differences between the two, but not quite in this way. It sort of physically articulates what I've been feeling. I'm not sure how I'll use it yet, but I'm going to. Somehow. I immediately begin to focus on how the man thinks. There is an order. A progression. A structure. And perhaps, most importantly, a *control*. Four-square is control. Order. A + B = A.B.

I take it to be this thought process which is expressed in the staging. I think about Andy's words as we work. Observing as we move through the rest of the afternoon. Looking for moments to push Andy's idea as far as I can. See what it reveals. Playing with moments. What if I give myself this one physical aspect to play with and focus on as we do the scene this time? I explore the language to find the corners of my thoughts.

Circles and squares. A circle can be a little wonky and still be a circle. There is some leeway before it becomes egg-shaped or oblong. A square *must* be precise. Unless the degrees are perfect, the edges won't meet or it will be a diamond. A square is all or nothing. It is or it isn't. Uncompromising. Precision is everything. I think back to my original thoughts on Aaron Burr. Precise. Deliberate. Economical. Ordered.

WEDNESDAY 25 OCTOBER

Something strange crept up on me today. Well, how it made me feel felt strange. The thought itself is not strange.

There's a little room at the top of the building which is always empty. I go in there to grab moments of practice when I can. I sit there. The sound of traffic and life floats outside.

I am set to play people who owned my ancestors. How obvious does that sound? Too obvious. Though it is true. Its truth is what shudders me. Washington, Hamilton, Burr, Franklin and Jefferson all profited from slavery. The historians will tell us that Burr and Hamilton did in fact represent enslaved people in court and various legal situations, but the fact remains.

In America, our brothers and sisters in the original cast were reclaiming and making history on many,

many levels. But the echo is no less resonant here in London. Most of us are here in this building because someone survived the very period we are exploring. Retrace our steps and it's a fact that some of us were on those ships at Yorktown. Some of us went up and down the Potomac. Some of us accompanied someone to the Constitutional Convention. Some of us were at Thomas Jefferson's place. Fought and died not just on the cotton field but also on the battlefield. Point is: this story is ours.

THURSDAY 26 OCTOBER

By the end of the week we will have reached the end of Act One. There are rumours there will be a run of the first half on Saturday. It's been a lonely week. Wake up in the dark. Head to the gym. Battle through the day. Come home in darkness. Steam my voice and try and take it all in. Also, relax and breathe. Bed. Bed in such a way that my brain is calm and at peace. Sleep is the most important time of all.

Everyone's tired. The dancing members of our company have information thrown at them that I can't even comprehend. I have so much to say and do, but they have just as much to sing and a thousand times more steps, shapes, lifts, moves to retain and execute.

I don't recall having had a rehearsal at this exact time of year. As the days are getting darker. Shorter. Go to work in darkness. Come home in darkness.

FRIDAY 27 OCTOBER

'Non-Stop' (no, really, *non-stop*).

The song which ends Act One. Once war is won, what happens? Life continues. Nations must be built. Rebuilt. Created. That which has been fought for must now be taken care of.

I had initially thought this song was about Aaron's anger at Alex. Once we spend time working on the number I see that the situation is more specifically about Aaron's frustration. The two most frequent words I use in the scene are 'Why' and 'How'. This is more active instantly. Attempting to find out how this Hamilton works. What is it that drives him to be so relentless?

It is becoming a question of obsession.

SATURDAY 28 OCTOBER

We run the first half of the show. Good. The value of running the whole thing is huge. Not there yet. I'm finding things. Fragments. My brain is too full of steps and staging and positions and cues. The

technical elements of the thing. Who the man is—
and, of course, no one really *is* anything. We are only
a series of hundreds of thousands, millions of
moments. Situations. Character is situation. Who
anyone *is* is only evidenced in whatever situation
they are in at any given moment.

So running the whole thing straight through is
massively useful and instructive. Stitching all those
fragments together starts to give you different
perspectives on the character. You see how the small
moments fit into the bigger picture. Close-up and
wide shot. A good performance uses both.

Jam and I are finding some things. The journey he
charts from young, scrappy and hungry kid to
statesman is something to behold.

★

By the end of the run, I am a zombie. Stagger out
into the fast-fading daylight and walk. Back across
the river to Charing Cross.

I read a while back that after Alexander's death and
the treason trial, Burr had escaped America and
spent some time in London. Hiding out in Craven
Street. Well, this evening as I crossed the river back
into town, I wandered up a different road to
Charing Cross. Recognised it as the street where the
Benjamin Franklin House/Museum is. Interesting
figure, Franklin. As one of the other Founding

Fathers, how come he's not in the show? Cos he was over here in Europe during the war, I guess. Angelica mentions him, though, at least.

I stop outside the house. Typically and beautifully Georgian. This one and all the other houses around it just as they would have been in 1776. It's more than easy to picture. Hence why they are able to make such an effective museum out of the house. Apart from the cars parked, you'd think you were in the eighteenth century. A little sign on the wall stating that Franklin lived and worked here.

I find myself staring at it. Then I suddenly come back to myself. Tired. Carry on up the road towards the station. At the end of the road I look up and see the street sign: 'Craven Street'. I turn back. This is the place where Burr lived in exile. Would make sense. Franklin was here.

I stand and stare. Aaron would have stood here and stared down the street and seen the river at the other end of it. I'm the only one in the street. It's night now. I stand there for a minute or so, trying to spot him in the darkness.

WEEK FIVE

MONDAY 30 OCTOBER

I don't take part in, but I do observe 'Cabinet Battle #1'. The thing I love most is the amount of observing. Watching. Hearing. These moments are loaded.

Washington gathers his fresh cabinet to get the new nation's finances in order. Hamilton proposes a national bank, but Jefferson thinks he's crazy and Madison thinks likewise. Once again, Alexander is in a situation where the people around him do not understand him. He is having trouble convincing them. His attack and passion seem to cloud his argument. This frustrates him. Jefferson takes full advantage.

In our very first meeting, Alexander recounts the story of getting into an argument with and punching the bursar. And here, once again, we hear him not being able to get his point across or achieve his aim because of his pace and drive and passion. Frustration and the threat of violence.

I see this. I see the bind he is in. This helps me going into 'The Room Where It Happens' and the line 'How're you gonna get your debt plan through?'

By the end of 'Cab Battle #1', Alexander is in a dire situation. Washington instructs him: 'You *have* to find a compromise.' Once again, Alexander sees the future, yet others ain't seeing it. Washington doesn't seem to clock it. I do. And it's not [*Unfinished line*]

TUESDAY 31 OCTOBER

'Say No to This.'

Just like in Shakespeare, tempo can inform you. The rhythm of what's written. Look at the patterns of what's being said. What repetitions? What does it suggest? What does it feel like? As Alexander tells us about cheating on his wife with his mistress Maria Reynolds, he repeats and repeats and repeats: 'Show me how to say no to this.' The repetition of what he claims he wants to avoid reveals the extent of his desires.

'Say No to This' starts with Burr. He addresses the audience and then hands the thing over to Alex. This moment feels immediately different to me. Different to all the other moments we've seen so far. Why? How? We play and I see. It is the first and only time that Burr doesn't walk towards the audience, his confidants. He enters at the back of the stage, stands under the street lamp and is carried forward by the revolve. Carried. Doesn't walk. I notice this is the only time this happens. What does this mean?

Then there's the music. Slower than we've heard it before. More deliberate. Low strings. The only time we have a hint or suggestion at something . . . what? Malice? Almost. Some enjoyment? A certain relish? Why? Why do I hand over to Alexander? Why do I stay to watch? Why do I leave when I do?

As Steph is staging the number, I suddenly remember something. I remember reading months ago about a court case Burr was involved in, and the whole situation suddenly makes sense. Or at least gives me something to try. Aaron watches and waits—and when he's got all he needs, he leaves. Satisfied.

WEDNESDAY 1 NOVEMBER

I had a dream last night. Or early this morning. My mother was in rehearsals but it wasn't Jerwood Space, it was somewhere different, but she was chatting to everyone and making everyone laugh. She wasn't sick, she was well. And it was lunch break. We were all hanging around. And just as Katy, our company manager, shouted that we were going to start again with 'Your Obedient Servant', she got up and walked out of the room.

★

After rehearsals I was packing up to go home. In the corridor outside the rehearsal room there's a window ledge where we all put our bags and coats. Only there aren't windows or glass. There are these big vertical wooden shutters which twist and open, letting in the air and light.

As I was putting my iPad in my bag, it slid off. I tried to grab it, but could only watch it go sailing off in slow motion straight into fresh air. We're at the top of the building. Five floors up. One second it's in my hand. The next—gone. I tiptoe over, look down, and see it five storeys below on the car-park concrete. I run down and its screen is smashed glass and twisted metal. Everything was on that. Photos, notes, rehearsal videos. Everything. Gone.

GREAT.

THURSDAY 2 NOVEMBER

We spend the entire day working on 'The Room Where It Happens'. We'd been told that the rehearsal photographer would be in the room today. Shots for the programme. Which I always loathe.

I snapped at Jam. I didn't mean to. He and Ash were joking around. They sort of egg each other on. Well, I almost snapped. I was pissed. He seems so unfazed by everything. He can goof around and have fun and get told off by Steph, and when his cue comes up—boom, he's right there. He doesn't drop a beat. He is fearless, I am fearful. It was a horrible and frustrating feeling to realise that what I felt was jealousy.

I remember when I saw the show in New York that when this number ended, the place came apart. It's the one.

Seeing it was one thing. Now I know more. I see it differently now. It is a play in itself. The *Rashomon* structure of the piece fascinates. Games are referenced a lot in the number. Specifically chess. The eighteenth century was called the 'Age of Reason', and this scene is an exercise in Reason. The idea that as humans we can feel whatever we like— but unless we can understand, comprehend, we are trapped. Like beasts.

So, as always, we go one step at a time.

It begins with Burr finding Alexander alone in the street one afternoon. They exchange pleasantries. Aaron enquiring about Alexander's progress with his financial plan. At which point they are interrupted by Madison and Jefferson, who approach and take Alexander off to their private dinner meeting. Leaving Aaron alone on the street. Excluded. Rejected. Not knowing what the fuck just happened. This is where the song starts. Six minutes later it ends with me jumping off the very dinner table I've been excluded from, with the entire company singing their faces off: 'I've *got* to be in the room where it happens.'

As we start to make our way through the number, Andy speaks again of the psychology of the scene: 'You know how, I'm sure, we've all had those moments where you find yourself standing in front of the mirror saying, "What am I doing? How did I get here? How did I get myself in this situation?" The idea that there is an ego which we have a dialogue with. It pushes us and tries to force us to do what it wants. Not always healthy or good decision-making, but making decisions nonetheless.'

The situation is someone not being present at a very particular event, trying to work out what went on at that event. In that room. At that dinner table. An intelligent mind trying to piece together what happened, and at the *same* time trying to work out *how* it happened and *why* he wasn't present.

The song proper starts out almost like the first line of a joke—'Two Virginians and an immigrant walk into a room.' An immigrant? Not twenty seconds ago I greeted Alexander with 'Mr Secretary'. This contrast tells me a lot. I'm enjoying learning how sharp the blade of Burr's humour is. I reckon Lin rightly serves up that, where Jefferson relies on funny, Burr weaponises wit. Which is all well and good but . . . The Virginians and the immigrant walk in the room foes, and come out with a compromise. How? I don't know. Because 'No one else is in the room where it happens.'

Okay. Piece together what evidence we do have. There is the retrospective account by Jefferson as to what happened, so Burr rewinds the song to this account of the seeds of the event: 'Alexander was on Washington's doorstep one day / In distress 'n disarray.' Concerned about how to make progress with his financial plan, rejected in Congress, Jeff suggests getting Alexander together with Madison to have dinner to talk through the situation. They could perhaps help each other out. Maybe. He offers to host the summit at his place. Dinner. Nice and easy, like. That's as far as Aaron's information from Jefferson can take us, so he then flips to the other player in the story, Madison.

Madison's situation is that he is frustrated with the ongoing problem of where to locate their new nation's new capital. Philadelphia? New York? The Virginians want Virginia, of course. And so we have two men with two very different problems. Alexander—capital, and Madison—*the* Capital. Both men, it turns out, *could* help the other. A compromise. Madison will help Hamilton get the votes for his financial plan *if* Hamilton will endorse Virginia for the capital.

Jefferson sees the opportunity and so, in Aaron's story, we flip back to Jefferson's version of events, suggesting he host the two frenemies for some dinner and a lil mutual back-scratching. So far, so good. However, that still doesn't tell us what actually *happened* in the room, only how the event came to be.

No one really knows how the
Parties get to yes.
The pieces that are sacrificed in
Ev'ry game of chess.

Aaron has come as far as he can go in piecing the puzzle together. As the dead ends begin to pile up, the frustration is forced up with them. For the first and only time in the play, I call out He who is ultimately responsible for all this: 'My God! In God we trust, / But we'll never really know what got discussed.' I want answers from Him too. But none come.

Therefore my gaze can only fall on the third player in this story: Alexander.

Alexander Hamilton!
What did they say to you to get you to sell New York
    City down the river?
Did Washington know about the dinner?
Was there presidential pressure to deliver?

Three rapid-fire questions with no gap for answers. Someone who always waits, now cannot wait for answers. Something is wrong. I stop suddenly. Lacamoire's arrangement slamming the brakes on to emphasise a new and terrible thought: 'Or did you know, even then, it doesn't matter where you put the U.S. capital?'

Now I'm filling in the blanks. Trying to put two and two together. More questions. No answers. Out of my frustration, Alexander's voice can now respond:

Cuz we'll have the banks,
We're in the same spot.

Aaron: 'You got more than you gave.'

But Alexander mocks me. Taking my 'got' and hurling it back at me. *Twice!*

And I wanted what I got.
When you got skin in the game, you stay in the
  game.
But you don't get a win unless you play in the game.
Oh, you get love for it. You get hate for it.
You get nothing if you . . .
Wait for it, wait for it, wait!

Mocking me with these, my own words, he lights a fuse to a powder keg labelled 'Injustice'.

The voices in my head now ringing louder and clearer. Now every voice on stage is taunting, haunting, piling up: 'You get nothing if you . . . Wait for it, wait for it, wait!' My own mantra flung back at me by Alexander and seemingly the whole world. Alexander holds up a kind of mirror. And I see/hear what?

From here on in, it's a conversation with the ego as much as with Alexander. And now for the first time in the song, exactly halfway through it, Aaron is referred to personally. At least maybe I see/hear it that way.

What do you want, Burr?
What do you want, Burr?
What do you want, Burr?

It feels like this last question mark becomes the final fish hook that rips off the door to the soul; a flash-reprised line of that pivotal moment back in the tavern at the start: 'If you stand for nothing, Burr, what'll you fall for?'—'What do you want?' No longer is the spotlight on Jefferson or Madison or Alexander—but on myself.

So I answer: 'I . . . '

That which was hinted at during 'Wait for It' is now expressed in full. Or rather, the thing itself, the *want*, forces its way up from the most hidden quarters of the soul, no longer content to stay concealed. The mask begins to slip and I rip it from my face.

As Andy says, 'It's one of those moments where the ego wins.' The desire comes charging up and erupts, not to the sound of blasts and fury, but to the delicate spider-web drops of Alex Lacamoire's fragile, quiet arrangement. As Sondheim says, 'There won't be trumpets.' And as Kander and Ebb echoed, 'It's a quiet thing.' When the character shifts his or her world, it is a quiet thing. The focus should be intense. Absolute. Terrifying. Tommy tells me to keep it as still as possible. This feels right. To admit what one wants—to one's self, to one's God, to the world—is both a shocking and an empowering thing.

We start with a man on stage, thinking he was going to try and piece together what took place during an event he wasn't permitted to be at, and through that, midway through the song, he realises, right there in front of the audience, that the reason he needs to know what occurred in that room is that he himself needs to be *in* that room. The metaphorical room. Where he is at present isn't acceptable. He needs to be somewhere else. This shocks him.

The trigger is Alexander's pointed statement: 'You get nothing if you . . . Wait for it, wait for it, wait!' Andy says, 'It's as if the man suddenly considers for the very first time in his life that everything he ever believed in or thought true could be wrong. Was it all wrong? And in that instant you realise. And you . . . what? Come apart.'

And through those cracks, I realise what it is I actually want. Or rather, I *express* what it is I want. The ego wins. And whispers:

I . . .
Wanna be in
The room where it happens.

The room where it happens.
I . . .
Wanna be in
The room where it happens . . .

The staging at this moment surrounds me with four
ladies. Arms raised. Hips towards me. Andy gives
them a little pelvic twitch. We are in the realm of
the ego, the libido, desire, hunger. My voice gets
louder. Its needs stronger. Standing now on the very
table I'd been excluded from, I jump up—and when
I land, the tablecloth is gone from beneath me—
and what's left? What else? A reflection. The
tabletop surface beneath the cloth is a mirror!

The leap down from the table isn't choreography
then. It comes with the line 'Dark as a tomb where
it happens.' This is someone desperately reaching
for freedom. To live in the light of his authentic self.
A caterpillar tearing open the cocoon and then:

I've got to be in the room . . .
I've got to be . . .
I've got to be . . .
Oh, I've got to be in the room where it happens . . .
I've got to be, I've gotta be, I've gotta be . . .

The repetition an incantation.

The iconic, climax choreography comes easy then,
especially when Andy explains it as the two sides of
us. The sophisticated, aristocratic, shoulder-height
finger flutters contrasted sharply with these base,

aggressive fist grabs. Both present within us and wrestling in the same human body.

★

We break, and Jam and I joke. He says it looks good and that my dancing wasn't as shit as he thought it would be.

Anyway, it's a start.

I'm reminded of what director Nick Hytner told us after the read-through on the first day of rehearsals of *Hamlet* at the National: 'What we are dealing with is the *us* which we keep within us, and the *us* which we show to the world. The conflict between them is constantly explored in this play.'

This comes to me now as I leave the room. This moment is the hinge of the entire story for Burr. After this moment, nothing can be the same. It's like when Hamlet comes back from England. Things are different. He is different. Somehow. After 'Room Where It Happens', Aaron is changed. Without that moment, he couldn't kill Alexander.

FRIDAY 3 NOVEMBER

I hardly say anything in 'Washington on Your Side'—but a massive amount happens for me.

It strikes me immediately when we start to put it on its feet that, rather than Aaron saying very little, the situation is in fact about him letting Jefferson say a lot. I start the song. With a surmise. A pretty noncommittal surmise. The man who has the word 'inimitable' in his vocabulary, here chooses the word 'nice'. And repeats it. The second time using two musical notes instead of one. Elongating the vowel for effect: 'It must be nice, it must be niiice to have Washington on your side.'

The word 'nice' might be hollow, but here it is far from empty. I'm a politician. Were this conversation to be repeated, there's nothing to incriminate me in 'nice'—but when I repeat the word, if I can sugar it with enough glint and stretch it to two syllables, it just might be enough to trigger Jefferson. Just enough to set him off and running. It is.

I talk with Jason. We've known each other for years. Worked together often. He's the senior member of the gang. There's a lot going on beneath the lyrics here so we talk, but only enough to say that for both characters, each goes through the situation believing they have the upper hand. Jeff through his manipulation of Burr. Burr knows otherwise. They have a common target. But who's going to make who fire the arrow?

One of the few things I do mention in the song is Hamilton's eyes.

Tommy watches intensely. Generally he talks a lot. He's brilliant at talking. I feel he likes me. We make each other laugh. But when I work, I feel his watch like a hawk. I'd imagine many people might observe that his strong trait is his ability to communicate, I'd be inclined to say that in fact it is listening. His ability to listen, hear, observe is pretty formidable and he does it by stealth. If there is a degree of Hamilton in Lin, there is certainly a degree of Burr in Tommy.

SATURDAY 4 NOVEMBER

I get the train to Charing Cross and walk along the river to rehearsals.

Saturdays at 9 a.m. there's no one walking down the South Bank. Empty paths, seagulls and lapping water.

Outside the National I stop and watch the little waves splash indifferently. Today we're doing 'We Know'.

I wish I knew.

I'm gazing out, nowhere in particular. A plastic bottle floats by. Ribena. In my view, from left to right. Doesn't stop to say hi. Just drifts off. To wherever it's going. Slowly and steadily. I watch it go. Further and further away.

That was this morning. Hours ago. I wonder where it is now. Somewhere on its journey.

MONDAY 6 NOVEMBER

Today, a strange day. Mondays often are the strangest of days. The previous week throws up many feelings and thoughts which all get digested on Sundays, then on Mondays your spirit asks, 'Okay, where are we now?'

'It's Quiet Uptown' is the number in the show which shook me most when I saw it in New York. It is the response in the show to the death of Alexander and Eliza's son Philip. It is a song/scene/moment which asks the question: How do you deal with loss? The loss of your child. The loss of trust. The loss of love. The loss of everything.

'If you see him in the street . . . '

As Burr, I do. I think all the characters do. Wrestling with the unimaginable. Burr and Theodosia's second daughter Sally died at the age of three.

There is one word which always snags on my insides when we're working: 'Forgiveness'.

Usually we think of forgiveness as something we offer or receive from others. Here, Lin tells us that in its truest form, it is something we must first *imagine*.

TUESDAY 7 NOVEMBER

'The Election of 1800.'

The end. My mind and heart are full. It's been a relentless month. Doesn't feel like a month. Learning. Trying. Stumbling. Falling. Searching. Discarding. Retrying. Playing. Finding things. Throwing things away.

As a cast, we know each other more now. Now I can look Jam in the eyes and see things there which were not there last time we did the scene. We can try things out knowing that the other will respond.

I think, somehow, that we both feel a very strong protectiveness over that which is unspoken between us. Whatever I'm doing, I couldn't do without him, and vice versa. Maybe we both have become more aware of that deep, strong bond between Hamilton and Burr, which throughout the events of their lives never seemed to break. Even after death. Some unspoken, unexamined thing which itself somehow lends a kind of terrible inevitability to Weehawken. Whatever it is, we are both aware of it. And therefore we let it do its thing. We talk a lot. But we don't get too close to that part. We understand each other and that's enough. It isn't for us to explain, so long as it's there.

I've heard people say that *Hamilton* is the story of two enemies. That's fine. I think it's nothing of the sort. There's nowhere to go if that were true. It is the story of two friends. Brothers. Only then does Weehawken become a place of tragedy. Only then does the duel break your heart.

Lin distils the historical actualities to the essential. In the Presidential Election of 1800, Hamilton rejects Burr. At the very moment I am about to achieve what is most important to me, Alexander destroys it. Betrayal.

We rehearse it and it feels like a knife in my heart. The climax of the song is staged so that Jam is directly behind me, way upstage. Made worse that I cannot see him. I hear it: 'Jefferson has my vote.'

By the time we get to Weehawken he has already aimed and fired at me a thousand times.

The more we piece it together, the more it makes sense. Not an intellectual sense. Deeper than that.

★

Like all great writers, with Lin you can trust his rhythms. I can feel it. Trust the flow and tempo of a path he's already trod and you'll see that there is a groove to guide you. If you're open to it. Same with Shakespeare. The writer has done the work and knows the secrets of sound and word combinations.

A tiny moment reveals itself. Seemingly tiny, at the start of 'The Election of 1800'. It is the last time Alexander and I meet on stage before the duel. I am on the campaign trail. The presidency in my sights. Handing out leaflets, 'I'm going door to door!' Both men at very different points in their life's journey. Alexander has fucked up with his marriage, lost his child, and been disgraced, but I'm on a roll. A surprised Alexander asks:

– You're openly campaigning?
– Sure!
– That's new.

Those last two words, the tiniest of sentences— 'That's new.'—could zip by unnoticed, but they are massively important. New ways are not usually associated with Burr. He has his way and sticks to it. What's changed?

All their lives, Alexander has been telling Aaron: Chase what you want. 'If you love this woman. Go get her' . . . 'What are you waiting for?' . . . 'What do you want, Burr?' . . . 'What do you want, Burr?' . . . 'What do you want?' . . .

And finally, here Burr can say: 'I'm chasing what I want. And you know what? . . . I learned that from you.'

As we rehearse it this time, Jam is surprised by this reply. Which in turn surprises me. Taken aback to discover the thought as the words are coming out of my mouth: 'I learned that from you.' I'm as surprised to hear this statement as he is. Revelation itself is not unusual to Burr. Revealing *is*.

At the start of rehearsals I had thought that this line was a parting shot. This time as we do it, though, I find myself expressing both surprise and genuine gratitude. What you've been telling me to do all these years I've finally done. And it's working for me. The moment can be played many ways, of course, but what if he simply means what he says? What if, for once, the famous Burr ambiguity has fallen away? He left it on the table in 'Room Where It Happens'.

This moment—'I learned that from you.'—is the button to the question that Hamilton barked in 'Room': 'What do you want, Burr?' But whereas in that moment I told the audience what I want, now I'm telling *him*. Without that moment in 'Room', I wouldn't be free now to chase what I want. Now, here on the campaign trail, I am doing just that. Thanks to Alexander.

This brief moment at the start of 'Election of 1800' strikes me as all the more important, considering that Hamilton will be well aware of it at the climax of the song as he is asked who gets his vote, effectively choosing the new President, and he proclaims, 'Jefferson has my vote!'

Cold-blooded.

All their adult lives, Hamilton has been telling Burr to go for what he wants. But Burr sticks to his guns. He waits. And waits. And waits. And then the moment he finally decides to follow Alexander's urging and go down this new and uncharted path, Alexander nails him. Hamilton nails Burr for doing the very thing he's always told him will do him good. And so, the end of their journey begins with letters written . . .

Dear Alexander, I am slow to anger . . .

And climaxes with satisfaction demanded . . .

Weehawken. Dawn.
Guns. Drawn.

WEDNESDAY 8 NOVEMBER

Something has been gnawing at me.

'The World Was Wide Enough.' Hamilton faces Burr—and death walks in.

Steph was finishing staging the previous song, 'Best of Wives and Best of Women'. The song is only twelve lines long. Funny, it's often the little things which reveal the big things.

It's the middle of the night before the duel. Alexander has got up and is writing in his office.

Eliza comes in and asks her husband to come back to sleep. Alexander is prepping for his meeting at dawn. *We* know what's coming. Eliza does not. She asks him again to come back to sleep. He doesn't.

– Well, I'm going back to sleep.
– Hey. Best of wives and best of women.

She goes. He leaves for the duel and they never speak again.

Standing by the window of the rehearsal room, watching the scene in the thin, late-afternoon sun, my parents come to my mind.

They met here in London. He at university, she training to be a nurse. They marry, start a family. By the time I'm born, his home country Zimbabwe is fighting its own war of independence with Britain. His brothers fight and die in the war, while he, the brilliant student, is set to return and be a part of the building of his new nation. But he gets sick as my sister and I are born, and in a few months is gone. Leaving her, best of wives, a widow.

Life is strange. I watch Jam and Shin as Alex and Eliza. He kisses her hand. And I wish my parents were here now. Perhaps things have been too crazy and busy for me to really sit with that thought before now. My father I never knew. But my mother. Well. There are moments when you just want to hear a voice. To talk to. To help. To encourage. Advise. To listen. To guide.

After rehearsals I do not go straight to the train as normal. Something pushes me along the river. Dark now. Cold. Past the Tate Modern. Past the National. Then suddenly a thought. Like a bullet.

Part of losing your parents is the real-world comprehension that you are now completely alone. No father. No mother. Just me. The sense of loss and being lost—total.
Alone.
Aaron Burr lost his mother, his father, his grandfather and his grandmother all in the space of twenty-four months.
What does that do to a child? Where does that push them?

In one of the biographies that I read, the writer mentions that Burr followed all of his male relations into theology, and halfway through his training left to study law. It is a tiny sentence. And I have only seen it specifically mentioned in this one book. It's always bugged me. Why halfway through? It's been lodged in my brain for a year now. Why? Why leave halfway through his training? In the middle.

As an actor, I want to imagine myself in the character's situation. Jam would have imagined what it was like being in that hurricane as a child on Nevis. He would have imagined being with his dying mother. What did she look like? How did she sound? What did she say?

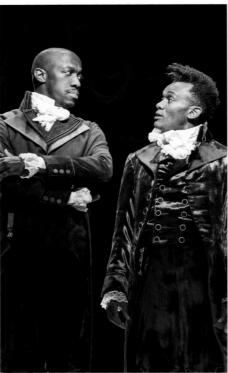

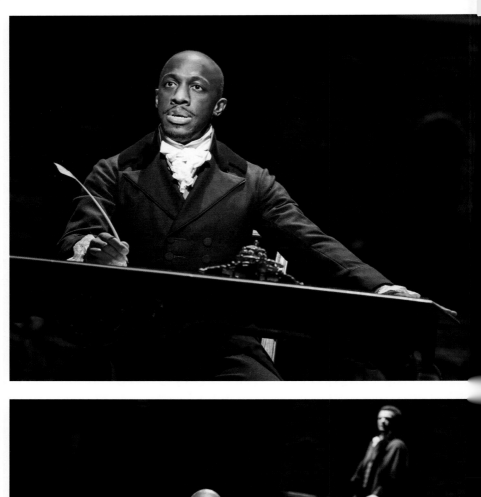

I need to learn what Burr's experiences are. What it was like.

So. What evidence?

Burr started training in theology and switches to law. But why halfway through? His father, grand-fathers—all extremely prominent, influential members of the church. There would have been pressure. An expectation that he is destined to be a preacher like them. But. It's not as if he balks at his familial tradition from the beginning and refuses right from childhood to even start his religious training. Neither does he complete his training and then end up in some other field. He stops *midway* and goes in a completely different direction.

As I look on the page it appears to me not as an intellectual idea but as a physical action. I trace it out in pencil on the page. He was doing one thing, moving in one direction, this way, and then all of a sudden he changes direction. Why?

I remember Andy: 'Hamilton is circles, Burr is squares.' I see the exact point of change of direction. A perfect right angle. But why does it occur? It is a small, passing sentence in a book and no reason is given.

And there, walking along the river after 'Best of Wives and Best of Women', something occurs to me.

In my own experience I had a moment where I found myself saying: 'Now I am alone. I have no one to guide me.'

Understandable. But in that moment I also heard myself feel: 'Now I am alone. There is no one to tell me what to do. There is no one telling me what to do.'

In the same moment exists the claustrophobia of loss and the liberty of possibility. Within that aloneness there is an unimaginable pain but also a freedom. Now your life is up to you.

What if?

What if Aaron had a similar moment? What if? Here he was. His father, grandfathers on both sides, uncles, great-grandfather, all theologians. In the eighteenth century, you do what your father has done. No question. Aaron Burr Jr will follow his father into the church. And so he goes. Until.

What if he felt as a very young man—'There is no one to show me what to do . . . It's down to *me*. I decide. I choose. I determine.' What if? What if that moment came right in the middle of theological training? What if one day, in the late-afternoon sun, he looked out of the window and said: 'There is no one to show me what to do. I decide.'

I see him grabbing his shit, walking out the door and never looking back. The world is his. It is wide enough. That is true liberation. True freedom. The freedom to walk your own path.

In that world, Burr might just be the most American of all the Founding Brothers. For what is more American than self-determination?
King George will not decide what we will be.
Father will not decide what I will be.
I decide.

I am the one thing in life I can control.

Aaron's realisation came at a high price then. Bought with tears and grief and aloneness and sorrows.

And therefore perhaps someone whose own self-determination, self-definition, was gained at such a high price might not react so well when bastard orphans try to determine what they are and what they are not.

'Jefferson has my vote . . . Jefferson has beliefs. Burr has none.'

Hamilton's words not only attack Aaron's political goals, they seek to crush the one thing in life I can control.

THURSDAY 9 NOVEMBER

We had our first run-through of the whole show. Somehow we have managed to receive, and absorb, the entirety of *Hamilton*. Each note, each step, each song, each moment, each thought, we have somehow managed to learn—and now we had to do the whole thing. There are mountains and there are mountains. It's been a journey to get this far for all of us. Everyone is knackered and on the edge of our immune systems, and yet here we are.

My voice is a little scratchy, but here we go.

I start the thing. A question. 'How does a bastard . . . ?'

The sentence is an incantation which provokes the whole thing. To start anything, a play, a song, to begin anything . . . I have been thinking recently of the act of saying anything. Even if all you had to say in life was 'How are you?' The breath that comes before the word is the important thing. It comes back, as always, to the act of breathing. Any good actor you see will have a powerful connection to their breathing. Any great speaker or spiritual person. The inhalation part of the act of breathing is incredibly powerful, but it is also the part we actors neglect. One only has to think of childbirth to contemplate the true power of the act of breathing.

Sat upstairs alone at lunchtime and it occurred to me. We don't even think about breathing, but there are, of course, two distinct actions. Neither is more important than the other. It feels like one thing because we're so used to it. I sat and observed for a while.

You breathe the air in and then the air goes out. I notice that more effort is used on the in-breath. You can feel the muscles have to pull the lungs out. Once the air is in, the walls feel like all they have to do is let gravity do its thing. Out goes the air. Then I thought—everything we ever say is on the out-breath. Every word we utter. Every speech. 'I have a dream . . . '"To be or not to be . . . '"That's one small step for man . . . ' The out-breath gets all of it. It sounds so obvious, but there it is.

I felt kind of sorry for the poor old in-breath for a second. It misses out. Until I realised that it does nothing of the sort. The out-breath carries the Word, yes, but the in-breath carries the Thought.

So after lunch, when we came to start the run, I tried to simply be aware of this.

Lac looks at me. Okay? I look around the room to make sure we're all ready. Nod. Let the breath drop in and . . .

FRIDAY 10 NOVEMBER

Every morning we come together and warm up. First physically, then vocally. For about half an hour. In America they don't do this. There, if they're due to start at 10 a.m., the actors arrive good to go and you launch straight into the first scene or number dead on 10. Here we come together and warm up together first. Likewise, when we move to the theatre for performance, it's the same thing. We gather an hour and a half before the show starts, warm up physically and vocally. Likewise, in America this doesn't happen. There you warm up in your own time. On your own buck.

The collective warm-up isn't simply to stretch your muscles or your voice. Its most important function, I think, is that of unifying the company. You greet each other, laugh, find out how each other slept and ultimately, as a group, focus your collective energy together to be able to tell that night's story. Together.

It also serves as a process of allowing the actors to get a lot of the personal stuff/energy out of the way beforehand so that it doesn't need to spill over into performance. It's a moment to deal with the outside world, our journeys to work, all our twenty-first-century-ness, get it all out, leave it at warm-up, so that we can focus as much of our attention as possible on the story we have to tell. That's the way I see it anyway.

As the weeks go by, we've got to know each other more, so the morning warm-ups get louder. Relationships have formed and humour is shared. Much laughing. Much joy. Teasing. Leslie Bowman and Obi being the chiefs. Throughout rehearsals, morning warm-up has become the funniest part of the day. A lot of funny people in this group and a lot of big personalities. A lot of energy. That collective energy can easily get unwieldy. We'll need it to get us all up the mountain, but it'll only get us there if it's focused.

Joy is the fuel of a theatre company's work—and this company works. Hard.

SATURDAY 11 NOVEMBER

Remembrance Day. We start with a minute's silence. And then for the rest of the morning in its wake, the room had a very particular quality. Intense.

Chris Jackson was in the room today. He played George Washington in the original Broadway production. Tommy had said Chris might be passing by as he was in town. And there he was. Before he'd even got here the energy in the room was charged. When he walked in, I scanned the room and there seemed to be people all over the place silently losing their minds. Trying to hold it together. The Americans were just as excited and happy to see him. Which was beautiful. For a second they were home.

When I saw the show in NY, Chris was playing Washington. His performance floored me. And now here he was. General Washington. But that was from our perspective. He himself simply walked in the room as Chris. Seemingly as one brother in a family. Quietly and with smiles. Sits and watches. His presence is not intimidating but supportive and encouraging. Good because there is work to do. A run-through to start. And this one needs to have moved on from the last. I was told by a director when I was at drama school: 'Each run-through, just pick a couple of things you want to work on. Don't try and do everything. Just focus on one or two aspects you want to work on that day and concentrate on achieving them. You'll improve quicker that way.'

I always liked that it's called a run-through. Not a stroll-through or a jog or a trot-through. *Run*-through, motherfuckers. Ain't nothing leisurely about this task. Yes, you want to come from a place of relaxation, but in the way an athlete does at an Olympic final. Run in this instance doesn't mean speed, it means purpose, momentum, forward movement, awareness.

At the same time, it's called a *play*—and we must never forget that's what we're here to do.

So I stand in my spot, the mid-afternoon sun on the back of my neck from the window behind me, and try to find that moment of stillness. Breathe. Lac nods at me. Ready? Scan the room. I nod back, let a breath drop, and here we go.

Jam is off today. Ash got to do the show. Ash is the alternate Hamilton. He's brilliant. Very funny and cheeky.

My eyes can't help but land on Chris Jackson during a few offstage moments. His eyes don't say judgement. They smile. The smile of 'Man, I've been where you guys are. I remember this. The sweat, the trying. Gasping for breath at the side of the stage, feeling like your lungs are about to burst. Being faced with any and every emotion in this scene or that song. What you're going through right now . . . I know exactly what that feels like. Keep going.'

Felt like his presence lifted and inspired us and he hadn't in fact said a word. Guess that's why the man played the part. Afterward there was chat and he said good things.

An important moment for us all, I feel. Some passing of some baton occurred, and coming from him it just made us see all the more how precious that baton really is.

WEEK SEVEN

MONDAY 13 NOVEMBER

Final week. More run-throughs. Next week we move to the theatre. Apparently Cameron will be in this week.

In musical theatre, actors are often referred to as Boys and Girls: 'The girls are called at 10.' 'The boys come on from stage-left.' 'The girls' dressing room.' 'I need all the boys over here, please.' 'We're auditioning ensemble girls tomorrow.' Regardless of how old you are. I always disliked it. Adults. Not children.

Infantilising actors always struck me as a way of keeping them powerless. These are not boys and girls; these are men and women. I suspect it came from ballet training, which begins at a very early age, and has seeped into all the performing arts.

Much of what I observe in the theatre is designed to keep the actors subservient. Powerless. Not just in musical theatre, all theatre. The actors are treated like children. Have to be kept in line. Not to be trusted on their own. Tolerated. Kept in their place.

The whole boys/girls thing is something I've never subscribed to.

It doesn't happen in this room, however. I'm grateful for it. In this room, the actors are referred to as men and women.

TUESDAY 14 NOVEMBER

Theodosia.

'You have my eyes . . . '

Aaron's eyes? Good/Not good?

Serious eyes? Older than my age? Mysterious eyes. Black eyes. Doll's eyes.

WEDNESDAY 15 NOVEMBER

Aaron.

Names reveal.

All of Burr's people were 'church'. On his father's and mother's side his forefathers were the most influential theologians in the American colonies. Elite men of God at the highest level of society.

I turn to the Scriptures.

In the Bible, Aaron was the elder brother of Moses. Yet their upbringings were very different. While

Moses was sent upstream in a basket, lifted from the rushes and grew up in the royal household, Aaron was raised with his kinsmen.

But when they grew up, Aaron and Moses were inseparable. Aaron accompanied his brother on his many visits to the Pharaoh demanding that Egypt let their people go. Aaron, with his brother, leads the Israelites to freedom out of Egypt to establish their new nation. He is with him all the way.

But.

In the story, once free and finally at the foot of Mount Sinai, when Moses goes up to receive the Ten Commandments from God, he chooses not to take Aaron with him. Aaron is left behind. While Moses alone ascends to receive the Word of the Father.

And no one else was in the room where it happened.

SATURDAY 18 NOVEMBER

Our final day in the rehearsal studio. My feelings, thoughts, emotions spinning. First, I am relieved to have made it here. I initially thought if I can get through the first week without being fired, I'll go from there. Step by step is the only way theatre works.

The rehearsal room starts out as a scary place. A place you know you'll be stretched and tested. A place where things good and bad will definitely happen. Like all places unknown, the deep dark woods, it is a place which is easy to be frightened of. The unknown is frightening to all humans. But slowly over the course of rehearsals, as the days turn to weeks, it becomes home. A place where you grow. Where you try things and discard things. A place where friendships have been formed. Fun had. Over there is where you always put your bag every morning. Over there is where you like to sit during breaks. You favour certain areas for reasons mysterious. You've been through things in this space. You've brought into the room all that you have in the service of whatever story you are trying to tell. The space transforms from unknown to known.

And now we prep ourselves to tell this story afresh for the last time here.

The room full of people from various departments. Maybe thirty in all. Packed really. The cast tired but raring to go. Pumped. We've made it thus far. In itself that's an achievement. Private tears aplenty, I'm sure. But also much laughter and plenty of jokes.

Feels like we've had a thousand run-throughs this week. I wonder whether the team thought we'd need more time. We're ready, man.

As always there's only so far you can go in a rehearsal room. Directors start saying the well-worn line: 'Now you just need an audience.' There's truth in it. Tommy doesn't say that, but we all feel it. What Tommy says to us is more accurate. That now we are *ready* for an audience.

It's by no means the end of the road. We ain't at the top of the mountain yet. It's a matter of—we've come as far as we can in this space. For the all-important element not present at the moment is the audience. There's no story without an audience. We have a story to tell but who are we telling it to?

So, we move. And the journey continues.

I always think if you can tell a story without lights, without costumes or big sets, just a room and some actors, then you really have a grasp on a story. This room has been a home and served us well.

Come Monday, it will once again be an empty room. Where something happened.

PART THREE

THEATRE

If it ain't ever going [...]
[...] me some thing you spend?
chasing. Things which elude and
weeks, and months, but ill
contrac. The essential better be
or it'll never be there. So the
built and the theatre gets buil[t]
We move into the theatre and
the characters welive been building
of the characters. These people.
[...]bly not weather the theatre
[...] will I be ready, not weather
be ready but weather Thea[tre]
I suppose the only thing you [...]
[...] brick.
[...] there inside is strong. I
[...]vas the theatre which [...]

MONDAY 20 NOVEMBER

The Victoria Palace has been closed for well over a year for a complete renovation. These old Victorian theatres are protected to within an inch of their lives. It's very rare that you see them changed. What's happening now at the Palace I've never seen. *Billy Elliot* was the last show here. Since then it's been shrouded in scaffolding like much of the rest of the immediate Victoria Station area.

Whenever I've seen Cameron in the last six months he's been anxious and passionate about the theatre. Our whole rehearsal period and the opening at the theatre was delayed because work on the theatre was still being carried out. The extent of the work being done on the building is staggering. A completely new auditorium, new stage, dressing rooms, new bars and new rehearsal space. Essentially a brand-new theatre.

Whispers rise: will the theatre be ready? These become the most frequently asked questions. The cast learn to bat them away. But as rehearsals speed along and time runs away, the urgency takes on a deeper, less humorous tone. The time for confident optimism passes. Just as for us performers the time passes when, during rehearsals we can say, 'Oh, I'll get that bit right. Next time.' There is a moment by which time if you ain't got it, it probably ain't ever gonna be there.

Of course, there are some things you spend the whole of the run chasing. Some moment. Some laugh. Some thought. Things which elude and evade you for weeks, even months. But I'm talking about the essential. The essential of the character better be there by week X or it'll never be there. So the character gets built—and the theatre gets built.

We make it into the theatre and take with us the characters we've been building. Our understanding of the characters. These people. I found myself not asking whether the theatre will be ready, but will I be ready? Only thing you can do is go brick by brick.

The theatre inside is stunning. They've been working round the clock, seven days a week. Inside and out. Workmen are everywhere. The sound of distant and nearby drilling. The percussion of creation. The theatre is a building site. Good. Shouldn't all theatre be?

I always marvel at Cameron's theatres, which he's lovingly and painstakingly renovated. The Noël Coward, the Novello, the Wyndham's . . . All brilliantly restored. This, he tells me at stage door, will be the 'jewel in the crown'. Walking around the theatre on day one of the tech I can fully believe him.

It appears new, but really it is old. It started out as a music hall. Designed, like so many of the great theatres in this country, by Frank Matcham. A lot has happened on this stage.

The dressing rooms are cool. I won't get to spend much time here during the show, but I like to get in to work early of an evening. Spaces are important. My room is opposite Jam's. His room is larger but mine's slightly closer to the stage. There's a little anteroom. Cameron tells me we both share it, but really I know it belongs to Jam cos it's physically attached to his room. Maybe Cameron suggests it to avoid any tension. There is none. As long as I have quiet and a shower I'm good to go. It's not quite quiet in the building yet, but it will be by the time we start to perform. Won't it?

Day one here and everyone is buzzing. You go into your dressing room and settle in. Costumes are on rails. We've had various fittings during rehearsals but now they are ready. All stitched and fitted and adjusted and perfect.

Everyone's buzzed and don't know if they want to spend more time checking out their own room or everyone else's. Every two seconds someone simultaneously knocks and pokes their head round the door. It's Cleve or Chrissy or Rachel. Checking out each other's new nests.

Over the dressing-room tannoys you can hear things happening in the auditorium. Lights are being set, crew shouting orders up into the flies, and musicians are going over things.

First things first, I go across the road to Boots and get water and Manuka honey.

TUESDAY 21 NOVEMBER

A lot of actors hate tech. All those long hours. Endless standing around. Going over the same bits, to no applause. Getting halfway through your panicked quick-change backstage only to hear over the tannoy: 'Okay, hold it, everyone. We're going back.' Endless stops and starts. People always say they find techs boring. I love tech.

I love how when you first walk out onto a new stage everything feels glaring and bright and loud and cavernous, but then over that first day or so your ears adjust to the space. And subsequently so does your balance. Your relationship to the new space has to be established. Stands to reason, you've just been in a rehearsal room for a month. When you stood at the 'front of the stage' in the rehearsal room, all that was in front of you was the unforgiving wall and half-a-dozen creatives looking pained. No audience laughs or gasps bounce back. Just the sound of your own voice.

Now, on the stage, the vastness of the auditorium is in front of you. Your voice travels out and up into the gods. It's a strange sensation. For the first few days of tech you feel as if you are in a vacuum. You have to adjust. I like that. I like finding it. It gives you new things. I like the fact that the first time you step out there it feels gross and exposing, but you know that soon it will feel like home. Just as the rehearsal room came to feel like home.

Also, I love grabbing time to explore the auditorium. Going out to the different levels to see what the audience will see. The experience from the stage is very different to the experience from the auditorium. With these Victorian theatres it's easy to forget how much space there is above your head. Perspective is very different in a large auditorium. In the rehearsal room, if you are watching from the front, the actors are big. You are close to them. The ceiling is maybe ten feet high. But on the stage, actors are tiny. They are further away and they are framed by the huge proscenium arch. Compared to which they are smaller.

★

Well, we've managed to get through the opening number.

The spacing is different somewhat from in Jerwood. I'll have to get used to it.

Three levels in the auditorium. Use them.

WEDNESDAY 22 NOVEMBER

The first thing I did when I got this part was buy all the books on Burr I could find. There aren't many. I'm sure more will be written now thanks to Lin and Ron Chernow. Washington has shitloads. Jefferson shitloads. Madison. Franklin. Hamilton. A lot. Burr—not so much. He does haunt the biographies of the other gents. He'll make cameos in Jefferson's books. Occasionally in Washington's. Adams'. Always portrayed in such a shady light so as to big up the hero in whoever's biography he is making a guest appearance. But anything written about him is useful. Especially contemporaneous accounts. Piece them together and faces start to appear.

One of the things which seemed to come up again and again as I started to research was Burr's attitude towards his clothes. Time and again, people seem to mention how specific and particular he was about his clothes and appearance. Interesting.

A person's attitude towards how they dress can reveal a lot. It always reveals something. This is a man who takes great care in how he presents himself. This is a man who always looks immaculate. I continue to imagine someone precise. Deliberate. Meticulous. Particular. Someone for whom details couldn't be more important.

Then, as I continued, I notice Hamilton seems to possess a similar attitude towards his own appearance. Many details about his fashion sense and fastidious wardrobe. It seems, more than any of the others, these two were known, not just for *what* they wore, but *how* they wore it. The utmost care was taken.

What if? What if this aspect is present not only in what he looks like but also what he sounds like too?

I notice that Laurens, Mulligan and Laff themselves use words in a very specific way and, as with all groups of mates, they share aspects of their linguistics. Theirs is a young, scrappy and hungry energy. Passion is foregrounded. They have something to say and an impatience to say it. Therefore one word can nudge the next one forward or even join it:

> – Two pints o' Sam Adams, but I'm workin' on
> three . . .
> – I am Hercules Mulligan,
> Up in it, lovin' it, yes I heard ya mother said 'Come again?'
> Lock up ya daughters and horses . . .

But where they employ rapid-fire monosyllabic words, the 'prodigy of Princeton college' spits *multi*syllabics:

> Inimitable.
> Deniability.

No one else in the play uses five- and six-syllable words as Burr does. As if he's saying, 'What you can say in a sentence, I can say in one word, motherfuckers.'

In-im-i-ta-ble.
De-ni-a-bil-i-ty.

Very rarely does he drop a letter off the end of a word.

The Sons of Liberty can because, maybe for them, what they are trying to express is the paramount thing. They are so genius that they can spit their bars in any number of ways. The Sons of Liberty don't feel limited by grammar. They take liberties with it and fashion their own. They are creators of new worlds after all. Whereas maybe I'm willing to wait and take the time it takes to express every corner of whatever it is I have to say:

Geniuses, lower your voices.
You keep out of trouble and you double your choices.

Burr knows that the thought is one thing, but the articulation of the thought is *everything*.

I find letters online. Burr would write to his daughter Theodosia as she grew up. She'd write back, and in his reply he would correct her previous letter. Make suggestions with her grammar or improvements to her imagery and economy. Again, you see someone who is precise, particular, meticulous, methodical, detailed, deliberate, exact.

Inimitable.

★

A couple of months ago, before rehearsals began, we had our first costume fittings. That's when I met Paul Tazewell, the show's brilliant costume designer. The large back room at Cameron's offices had been transformed into a sort of Alice in Wonderland of materials and fabrics and clothes rails and sketches and boxes of hats and boots. Beautiful work-in-progress things, which would somehow be transformed into costumes, lay on every surface.

I was draped in what I recognised would become my first Act One jacket. I knew this because of the rich wine colour of the material. It had pins in it and only one sleeve and no real collar and no lining and bits flapping loosely. And I watched Paul, quiet and attentive, squint and tilt his head, walk round me, move a bit of material here, mark it, pinch a bit at the shoulder and pin it there, step back, adjust the right cuff, re-pin something at the side, make me raise my arm, nod, make me lower my arm, adjust something else, ask me how it felt, squint, ask for this lapel or that cuff to be moved ever so slightly. We're talking millimetres. A stitch's width. It was hard for me to picture the finished thing, but he could see it all.

Most of us look and see a jacket. Others see a million tiny stitches. Each one vital and contributing to the success of the whole. Without that stitch it is something else. Without that detail it is incomplete.

I want to use that. For the way Aaron moves, thinks, speaks. *Is*. Because he knows. He knows that if one is going to say the word 'Weehawken', then the 'n' is as important to that word as a button on a cuff on a coat.

THURSDAY 23 NOVEMBER

Anna Wintour, editor-in-chief of *Vogue*, was sat in the front row with an entourage for most of the afternoon as we teched. She knows Tommy and Lin, I guess. Super-friendly and very excited and encouraging. Afterwards I realised that I had just had my first encounter with a '*Ham Fan*'.

FRIDAY 24 NOVEMBER

The Acting Natural and Sprightly.

I discovered that Burr, after politics and bloodshed, in exile, occasionally went to the theatre. In his own journal he tells us about one such experience in Europe:

> To the theatre. A comedy and farce in Swedish. Silence. Order. Not one laugh, except Hosack's. Less buffoonery than in England or the United States. The acting natural and sprightly. Curtain continues up till the end of the play, and again from the beginning to the end of the farce. No change of scene. The same throughout the whole performance. The orchestra good, and one of the women a very fine voice. Not a light except on the stage; but

between the pieces a large lustre, with about twenty Argand lamps, let down from the ceiling, so that we could then see each other. No noise, even between the pieces, except cheerful talk, in the tone of common conversation. The dresses very good. No handsome or elegant women, but it is said that there is one who did not appear. A box ticket is a rix-dollar; but the highest places (they were all taken) a dollar banco. At home a little past 10. Still broad daylight.

Note to self: act natural and sprightly.

SATURDAY 25 NOVEMBER

'Sitzprobe' in German means 'seated rehearsal'. Known to be far and away the most exciting moment of the whole rehearsal process, the sitzprobe is when the orchestra and cast meet for the first time to run through the whole score together. Sometimes it takes place on the stage of the theatre, or the rehearsal room, but most often it takes place at a special sound stage somewhere.

Lac told me before rehearsals that they got Abbey Road Studios for our sitzprobe. Then rehearsals got delayed and we lost our slot because the space was already booked for the following weeks. So this time we have our sitzprobe at a music sound stage on an industrial estate in Bermondsey. A huge, six-floored venue where, judging by the posters on the walls, most of the massive live bands of the eighties and nineties rehearsed for their big arena tours.

We've been singing the score for weeks, but with the rehearsal piano and some programmed beats to give us a feel. Now we hear the full orchestra for the first time.

Chairs are spread out across the far end of the room. Music stands and mics in front of each. And in front of us, facing us, the orchestra is sat. Ready. Good to see Beadle again. We haven't seen our musical director much this week. He's been working the band. He looks like it's been a full-on few days. He looks happy to see us, though. Funny, in these circumstances anything familiar you cling to. There's a shitload to do, but a quick smile can fuel an hour.

Everyone is excited. Just the fact that we are out of Jerwood Space is bliss. No staging, no moves, no choreography, just stand and sing. Boom.

Vocally you want to be able to throw down, but at the same time you don't wanna burn up. Nothing to prove here. Just hear and fit with the orchestra.

Lac buzzing about the massive room driving the whole thing. There are maybe a hundred people in the room. Hearing Lac's arrangements for the first time is sick. Finally get to hear that banjo in 'Room Where It Happens'. Funky as fuck.

Strings. Things. Trumpet stings
Triangle '*tings*'
The kick drum in the opening

King George's harpsichords
The drum fill into 'Schuylers'
Cellos. Violins. Viola
Piano licks in 'What'd I Miss?'
Kick Drum Boom 'Where It Happens'
Banjos. Voices. Beats. Scratches
Cannons. Samples. Horses. Drum patches.

MONDAY 27 NOVEMBER

I snuck out front to catch a moment of 'Yorktown'. Those people look like superheroes on that stage!

Then in the stalls, talking to Nevin Steinberg about his sound design. When I saw it in NY I was stunned by the sound. How they can get such boom without it melting the audience's ears. Most rock/pop shows whack everything up to 11 and it can be hard to hear what is being said. With this show you can *feel* every note but also *hear* every word. I asked Nevin about it. Those famous refrigerator-sized speakers I've read about. Busy as he is, he didn't seem annoyed by my curiosity. We had a good chat.

TUESDAY 28 NOVEMBER

The Prince.

We were all standing round on stage this evening, waiting for lights to be adjusted. Dinner break was just about to be called. Suddenly from the stage-right wing, Prince Harry walked quietly on stage. Everyone stopped. For a second people just stared. He raised his hand to his face, slowly lifted off his cardboard tourist mask, and it was Lin-Manuel. The whole place lost its shit. General screaming, cheering, jumping, laughing, hugging. Gabriel Mokake did a death drop.

Typical of Tommy to keep it secret. He hadn't said a word. He knew that it was an important moment. For us all. He knew that this was more than meeting the now very famous creator of the show. Lin is one of us. At least he behaves that way. He is an actor and he knows what it's like. Like Chris Jackson, he knows one hundred per cent what we are experiencing. And that is the level on which he responds to us. He walked into the place with love. Available and free.

It was as if he was saying, 'Yeah, outside I might be the prince of all of this, but behind that, underneath, in here, on this stage, I'm one of you.'

WEDNESDAY 29 NOVEMBER

Jefferson's Footsteps.

At the start of Act Two we are introduced to Thomas Jefferson who's been over in Europe during the war years. I come on at the start as per, welcome my confidants back to the second half of the show, and set the stage for Thomas. Who enters at the top of the high, movable wooden staircase, and saunters down to take his place centre-stage in the proceedings. I start the song at the front of the stage and by the time I hand over to him thirty seconds later I am at the top of the wooden stairs at the back of the stage. Therefore. I have to get to the top of the stairs while singing. Backwards.

After dinner we get to this point in the proceedings. We haven't had the staircase in rehearsals obviously. Steph asks me if I'd like time. I most definitely would. She tells me that each Burr has their own way of getting to and up the stairs. Cool.

I try. First time, I trip. Second time, I trip. Now, either I can back up towards the bottom of the steps or find a moment to turn into them so that I am still facing the audience. I need to try and find a way to get to the foot of the steps with as little time as possible with my back to the audience. Not because I want them to see my pretty face but because I am singing—and words are important. I always feel that in a theatre, an audience hears with their eyes as well as with their ears. Sometimes, if an audience can't see your face, and more specifically your mouth, then they feel they cannot hear what has been said. So. If I'm going to turn, it needs to be quick and between sentences. Somewhere.

I try again. And again. Not the right place. Frustration. I try again. Find a spot. After *that* full stop. Okay. Now, getting *up* the stairs. I keep catching my heel on the step as I try to go up backwards. Fuck it. Go back down to the first step. Have another go. Slower. Better. Getting up is not really the problem, so much as I need to make it look as if I'm not thinking about it. Needs to look effortless. Burr is neither clumsy nor awkward. It needs to look like it sounds. I stop. I go up forwards and count each step. Twelve. Okay, so on the twelfth step I am on the top. Back down to the bottom. Go again. Backwards. Now I can move more confidently. Not quite. I have to sing. I can't be counting steps while I'm singing. I know I'll get used to it and in two weeks' time will be able to do it with my eyes closed. But now! Try again. It's not okay to count steps and sing. I'm running out of time. Things look like we're ready to move on. It's not even my damn number. There's a whole stage of my brothers and sisters getting ready to kick and buck their way all around the stage, and Jason is about to do splits and all sorts. All I have to do is walk my ass up a flight of stairs backwards. It has to be effortless. Or appear so. So effortless that the audience don't even really notice it. I remember when I saw the show in NY how moved I was during it when I felt that all of a sudden something had just *happened*. In front of our eyes. Miraculously. That's what it needs to be. Something miraculous should happen. I'm talking to them and all of a sudden . . . there's Thomas Jefferson! Practice. Practice and more practice.

The miraculous only happens with repetition, work and patience.

THURSDAY 30 NOVEMBER

Knock. Paul Tazewell came in the dressing room with the rest of the wardrobe department. Apparently I've lost weight, so adjustments need to be made.

I love these clothes. For the simple reason that they are not costumes. Costumes are things which belong to someone else. These clothes feel like mine. They don't feel like something someone else has chosen for me to put on. They feel like I went through and chose them. That colour. That button. That cuff. More importantly, clothes inform. They tell you how to walk, sit, breathe. How to turn your head. Especially if they are period clothes. Sweatpants and T-shirts give freedom but not much else. Which is fine. These clothes, however, hold the body. From the boot to the chin, everything is structured. Lifted. Held in place. In these clothes it is impossible to slouch. The head is lifted.

I decide to go with this as far as I can. In rehearsals I had been standing naturally as I had seen in images of the time. One foot resting slightly in front of the other. We all know that posture. As soon as we have our clothes, though, this doesn't feel right. For me. I play around as we tech and find myself naturally standing either with my feet parallel or together. Neither one in front of the other. This comes from the entirety of what I'm wearing. Everything encourages you to stand up straight. And now, lack of symmetry starts to bug me as I stand, move, sit. Just as his thoughts and words must be deliberate and ordered, so too must his movement. Now I notice that I start to stand with both my hands behind my back. Not something I would ordinarily do in life. But here . . . He stands straighter than I do. I notice he develops this little habit of adjusting the right cuff. As I'm listening to Jefferson or Hamilton. A little tic. Keep that. I think about how he would have had to present himself as a soldier and what of that would have stuck.

SATURDAY 2 DECEMBER

In three days' time we'll have our first audience.

Every single member of the company is exhausted. The day starts slightly later now, but tech goes on well into the night. The auditorium and stage have no windows. You never quite know what time it is. Time begins to bend. You arrive in the morning and people say to each other, 'Weren't we just here? Didn't I just see you two minutes ago?'

We need a break, but that ain't happening. We're halfway up a mountain. I'd say there isn't a single member of the company who isn't physically, vocally, mentally, emotionally and psychologically smashed.

Obi is going through it. As is Rachel. Cleve and Tarinn bounce through, up in it, lovin' it. Jam is on great form, all things considered. All things being *Hamilton* and a new baby. Bowdiddy and I were reminiscing about rehearsals today. Seems like a lifetime ago. Now we are further along the trail.

We ran the show from start to finish in full costume with lights and sound every day this week. Jam had one of them off while Ash took a turn, but for all it's been a full, full week. There were times when I wondered if I would make it to the end of the week, but somewhere in the sitzprobe I told myself, or it felt like a voice told me: Relax. Give in. Let go. Believe in what you've done. Don't be subject to the doubts which have been threatening to hold you back. Just have the strength to let them float away like so many balloons into the blue winter sky. Relinquish them. Let them loose. At one point they might have been in some way useful—they focused you and made you not take anything for granted— but now they are empty and useless. And if you drag them behind you, you'll never get up this mountain.

PART FOUR

PERFORMANCE

...ner Alex's question. Why? I could
...care. Because surely his first occ...
...has snagged his mind. What ar...
...? "What are you waiting for?"
...the say WAIT FOR IT. That's ~~not~~
...don't he answer Alex? Austin He called ...
Alex. That would be an answer and
... But ~~that~~ not what happens. He lets
... eye lets me hear this sentence ...
...uncof art before - "I will now ca...
~~the right~~ ~~was~~ Th
~~that~~ an extraordinary thing for Alexad
...undoubted you". ~~The~~ young man che "
...drafted eighth. The man who Aaro...
"Scary for eg both he can see his had
...my first ~~meeting~~ encounter tells me - "
...trated course of study." Who's -
...go to King's College." who also he

Our first preview.

Last night's open dress rehearsal was a packed house full of friends, family and peers. It was like a rock gig. Tommy and Lin and Cameron all gave a speech at the start and then the thing began.

It was one of those events that becomes an out-of-body experience. You are sort of floating above the whole thing. A very mysterious feeling. You really want to be a hundred per cent *in* yourself. Present. But the nature of the situation is bigger than that. On a ship you can stand as still as you like, you are still on the ocean.

Last night, from the moment the house lights went down and I walked out and spoke the first lines, it was a Southern Baptist revival meeting.

Tonight, however, it was our first paying audience. Who've all waited so long to be able to see this show. It was an extraordinary atmosphere. No speeches, just house lights down, and out I step into the empty space to speak the first words of the piece.

The best times in theatre are when the audience is unified, when a thousand people or ten people are all somehow experiencing the same thing simultaneously. Different thoughts and feelings and responses but the attention is unified. That happened tonight. They went crazy. It's hard to describe what it felt like.

It was as if they were so ready to hear this story and go on this journey, all we had to do was steer. Be open to that willingness. You could actually *hear* their attention. A kind of static. Tommy had warned us, after last night, not to let the audience carry the whole thing away in their excitement. A thousand people's energy is a lot to harness.

When the opening number finished, the place exploded. Different, though, to last night's open dress. Last night they were people we knew. Friends and family. They were there for *us*, tonight they were there for the show. I've never heard a sound like that. The audience were hungry. Tickets have been on sale for almost a year. They know this show backwards and those folk were *ready*. People in *Ham* T-shirts. Groups of girls clutching each other. There was one young kid in full costume. When Cleve came on, they screamed. When Jase came on, they screamed. When Tarinn came on, they screamed. When Westman came on and said, 'Alexander Hamilton. My name is Alexander Hamilton', the whole room lost its collective mind.

Looking up at us from the orchestra pit, Beadle had to just hold the band and wait. They were still screaming as we began 'Aaron Burr, Sir'. As Jam and I started the number, there was a fire look in his eye, like 'What the fuck is going on?' We were in danger of being overwhelmed. So as we then turned into the tavern, I squeezed his shoulder and found myself telling myself quick: Okay, keep it together. Breathe. Remember what Tommy said. What are we here to do?

In this piece, Lin has Burr come out and tell his confidants: 'You *think* you know the story, but you don't know the whole story.' Right then. There you go. My task is Burr's.

The joy of the whole thing comes from looking into your fellow actors' eyes as the story unfolds. Hearing them. Knowing the struggles we've faced and still face. The play is, among other things, about a group of people struggling to survive—and in many ways our company reflects that. Somehow there is great, clear power in the *us* of it all over the *me* of it all. Everywhere you turn onstage there is someone doing their thing. Telling the story. Fighting their cause. Making their turn. Singing that harmony just as Lac wanted. You step off the turntable and someone is there to replace you. The space you step into vacated by someone else. Eighteenth-century clockwork with a twenty-first-century alarm.

Massive crowd outside afterwards. It's cold but people wait for autographs and pics, screaming and still singing the songs. It stuns me for a second, but I'm still pretty gassed from the show, so it's actually a mad kind of fun.

Then there are drinks in the restaurant next to the theatre. None for me. I turn into the busy bar and there were Lin and Cameron. Beaming. 'Told you it would be crazy,' Lin shouted over the noise. 'Welcome to the roller coaster.'

THURSDAY 7 DECEMBER

Woke up this morning after last night's first preview and wondered for a second or two if it had in fact actually happened. Or did I dream it?

It feels like air to have people to tell the story to. I spend half the show talking to them.

Adrenaline sweeps you along through firsts. First days at school. First dates. First performances. Then there is the next day. What do you do the day after? No one ever tells you that. I'm on the train coming in. Thinking about the *day afters*.

Aaron Burr opened his eyes the day after Weehawken. For a second or two you forget. Your eyes are just adjusting to the light. Then you are fully awake. And the previous day exists once more and you say to yourself: 'Now what?'

FRIDAY 8 DECEMBER

We come in every day, early, and work on the show. What we weren't able to nail last night we work on today. We meet on stage. Steph will give us notes. Lac will give us notes. Tommy will give us notes. We work on things. That bit in the opening. That section in 'Non-Stop'.

Often, before you get the note, you already know it's coming. You were there. You know you messed up or were in the wrong place for that line. You write it down in what has become a sort of weird hieroglyphic shorthand, and try and get it right today.

1. Opening—3 Laurens' verse.
2. Move on 'name'—What's your name, man. Don't walk at the start.
3. Don't hold book out on 'Clerking. Working.' Johnny.
4. 'Schuyler Sisters'—Move on drums. Step on drum fill.
5. 'Helpless'—Washington salute back against wall. Stay back.
6. Ten Duel—'Number 5'. Let Jade and Curtis go first.
7. 'Yorktown'—Pass Alex then turn back and see him.

SATURDAY 9 DECEMBER

The theatre takes on the atmosphere of a furnace. A sort of collective heat is generated. Each person contributes to it, and each day we come in and see the same faces, the same walls, the same black-void auditorium. The same glare of humming light. The same smell of new carpet and fresh wallpaper. The same tired eyes, the same full hearts.

The repetition combined with the fatigue produces a sensation not unlike being at sea. A sort of perpetual but eventually familiar floating.

But with that, the work needs to be done. The words spoken, the songs sung. The thing has to be forged and so, each morning, the company comes in and once again does battle with that day's dragon. In the furnace.

We don't snap at each other and no one really snaps at us. It isn't a toxic atmosphere. Far from it. The creative team are jovial and good-humoured. Have been throughout this whole thing. It's simply intense. Lin-Manuel is always close by, fizzing about something out in the dark auditorium.

Helena Bonham Carter was in the auditorium with him as we worked yesterday and then she came and saw the show with her fam in the evening. Beautiful and very funny. She said we must all be knackered, so this afternoon she came into my dressing room with this amazing tea that looked like strips of dried tree bark. 'You lot will need good strong immune systems. This was a godsend during *Sweeney Todd*.'

She instructed me how to make the tea, gave me some for Jam, and was gone. I made some and took it through to him. Tasted amazing.

★

One of the things which gets me most about this whole thing is how we end the night. It's something I haven't seen written about, but we've had three shows so far in front of three audiences, and it's moved me every night.

The show ends and Tommy has us all walk to the front of the stage, hold hands and bow. All of us. Together. No individual bows. We step forward and acknowledge the audience as one.

SUNDAY 10 DECEMBER

I've been wrestling with 'Wait for It'. I know what I feel it should be, but can't get there. Yet. It is a deceptive moment. What actually is going on in that moment? What am I saying? What am I trying to do?

During tech, when we sang the whole number through first time, Lac wasn't happy, I could tell.

I was pitching it too small. Maybe. Not sure. Tech is about adjusting to the auditorium. The rehearsal room was big, but smaller than the auditorium. You have to adjust. Lac's always been very cool with what I've been doing so this made me freeze. Well, suck it up, boy. This is why we're here. Tommy watching like a hawk. Arms folded but eyes open. Andy and Steph giving notes to everyone around me, and me—centre-stage—doing what? Voice from the darkness: 'Okay, when we go back we'll pick it up again from the top of "Wait for It".'

Okay. Rewind.

When I saw the show in NY, this moment shook me deep. Listening to the score is one thing. *Seeing* the story is another. I was struck by the timing of the moment. I remember feeling that the song came just at the precise moment I found myself thinking, 'What about Burr?'

Watching the show, we, the audience, have just been treated to twenty minutes of New York society. General Washington and his brewing army, then the Schuyler family and Manhattan's finest movers and shakers. We see Alexander court, try his hand, fall in love and get married. We see Angelica helplessly unsatisfied with her sacrifice. We see the Sons of Liberty rally, support their friend, and gear for war. But what of Burr?

He's been there throughout. Guiding us through, but what does he feel? Where's he at? Lin times it perfectly so that the audience is feeling exactly what the characters in the play are feeling at precisely the same moment. What's Burr's deal? This is when the alchemist Miranda drops 'Wait for It'. He made us wait. And we are ready.

As Aaron, I know that this is my opportunity to talk to the audience. My confessors. For Burr, there are two relationships: with Alexander and with the audience. Apart from Alex, the only people he trusts are the audience. The whole story is a confession and there is zero point lying to your confessor. Everything Burr tells the audience, he does so in order to make them understand what led him to pull a trigger. You understand me as the villain— well, here's why I am not. He doesn't ask for forgiveness, but understanding. So the song must feel a totally open and honest moment. Bare. Exposed. Tommy had said keep it interior. Don't sing it to the audience too much. But as we stage it, I don't feel that. I feel it's a vital moment to share with them. Everything I say I already know. I know Theodosia writes to me every day. I know who my father and mother were. So who am I talking to? My friends. Why am I telling them?

Okay. Rewind.

The most important thing in a song is what triggers it. What impulse makes the character want to sing?

Need to sing? What kicks them off? What is it they are trying to address? I find if you are struggling with a line or thought, the answer will always be in what you've heard. In someone else's line. So what's been said?

After 'Satisfied' we get 'The Story of Tonight (Reprise)'. The fellas bowl on, drunk from festivities. Ribbing and celebrating the newly married Alexander and excited at the prospect of war, glory and freedom. As actors we are told where we enter, move to and stand, but the interesting and vital thing to discover for yourself is why.

Aaron arrives on stage just after them. Entering from the same place they did. As we play, I find an important moment. He doesn't just walk in and walk over to the guys. There is a specific moment where Aaron enters, the first thing he sees is that he isn't included. They are there and I am here. Separate. But on whose terms? I know that I can't compete with the Sons of Liberty, so I deliberately stand apart. Another important beat. What if I choose my own space in the room to stand, knowing that Alexander will come to me? Which he does. Now I have separated myself from the group and we can talk. But what do I need to say?

The fellas persist and come crashing into our space. Laurens getting a little too close for comfort. Jam's Alex is sensitive and smart enough to sense that I have something to say—or else he wouldn't have come over—he's no pushover. Dismisses the guys and we are alone. Straight away he congratulates me on my recent promotion to Lieutenant Colonel, and says:

– I wish I had your command instead of manning George's journal.
– No, you don't.
– Yes, I do.

Throughout their lives it's always about which one is ahead at any given moment. Who's achieved what? Who's been promoted? Who's got the family? During 'Helpless' it was Alexander. Got Washington's right hand. Got Eliza's hand, which means he's in with Old Man Schuyler and all his political clout. He's got it all. But now Aaron has been busy too. Lieutenant Colonel no less. *And* he's in love. *But* she's married. *And* it's the wife of an enemy officer. So . . . he'll wait. First things first: the war. If I can get through that, the rest will fall into place. But Hamilton says:

– 'I will never understand you. If you love this woman, go get her. What are you waiting for?' He asks.
– 'I'll see you on the other side of the war.' Is the reply.

Burr does not answer Alexander's question. Why not? He could. But he doesn't. Why? Because. Because something has just occurred to him. Something has snagged his mind. What was it Alex just said? 'What are you waiting for?' Okay, I'll explain it to him in the song 'Wait for It'. But that's not what happens. Why doesn't he answer Alex's question? He could sing 'Wait for It' *to* Alexander. That would be an answer and it would make sense. But that's not what happens. He shakes his friend's hand and lets him go. Something in Jam's eye and delivery, though, lets me hear this little sentence at the *start* of the phrase which I haven't thought too much about before. 'I will never understand you.' Interesting. To the right ears it is an extraordinary thing for Alexander Hamilton to say: 'I will never understand you.'

The young man who makes it his mission to understand everything. The man who Aaron tells us spends his time 'Scammin' for every book he can get his hands on'. Who, in our first encounter, tells me: 'I was seeking an accelerated course of study.' Who's gonna 'get a scholarship to King's College'. Who, when he was seventeen and a hurricane destroyed his town, 'Wrote my way out'. Who 'Wrote everything down far as I could see'. Who 'Wrote my way out of hell'. Who 'Wrote my way to revolution'. Who 'Wrote about the Constitution and defended it well'. Who 'Wrote financial systems into existence'. Who 'When my prayers to God were met with indifference, I picked up a pen, I WROTE MY OWN DELIVERANCE.' This is not a man who says 'I will never understand' easily.

And however Alexander chooses to say it, it is enough in that tiny moment for me, in one instant, to be made aware of the fundamental differences between us. It is an important realisation. What attracts Aaron to Alexander to begin with was what they have in common. Here, in this moment, maybe I scratch out what is the essential difference between them. What Alexander sees as a flaw in Burr's character, Aaron knows is a strength. In fact, what if Alexander here reveals a flaw in his own make-up? His inability to see past the immediate. His inability to see things from any perspective other than his own. Aaron clocks this and knows he has a choice about which way he himself is going to go.

And so. I share with the audience. My way, which Alex cannot understand, is the best way. And here's why: 'Theodosia writes me a letter ev'ry day . . . I'm willing to wait for it.'

But. Lin is a genius. Make no mistake. He could have left it at that. Certainly it would still be great. But what makes it feel like such a human moment is that the writer balances certainty with doubt. Two-thirds of the way through the song, I stop: 'What is it like in his shoes?'

What if I'm wrong? What if he's right? What if? What if someone who's spent their entire life being certain suddenly has a flicker of a moment? What if? Such is the force of Alexander Hamilton's own conviction/energy. I can't imagine anyone else in the play convincing Burr to question himself. No chance. But Hamilton . . .

'What is it like in his shoes?' It stops me dead. What if this is the first moment of doubt I've ever had? I'm reminded of Hamlet. There is much Shakespeare in this story. 'To be or not to be . . . '—halfway through the speech, Hamlet stops:

> To sleep: perchance to dream: ay, there's the rub;
> For in that sleep of death what dreams may come
> When we have shuffled off this mortal coil,
> Must give us pause.

Right there, in that moment, Hamlet stumbles on something he's not quite thought of before. So it is with Burr. What if?

He reasons it through in the presence of his confessors and decides what he must do. Lin's lyric here is stunning. At this pivotal moment, he gives Burr three sentences with no gap for a breath. A runaway train of thought. They must be done in one breath so that the audience doesn't know which way you are going to go. Perhaps Burr *has* been swayed by Alexander. Perhaps he *does* see and accept that Hamilton's way is right. Perhaps he *does* buckle and turn. Could go either way. Perhaps he *should* go get Theodosia. Perhaps he *should* go get it. Perhaps he *should* be more like Alexander. One breath.

> He changes the game.
> He plays and he raises the stakes.
> And if there's a reason
> He seems to thrive when so few survive,
>   then goddamnit –
> I'm willing to . . . wait for it.

The decision is revealed only at the very last moment.

This feels right. I'll try it. We shall see. After, Tommy says something brilliant: 'As he finishes the song, resolves all he has to say, then he very carefully and deliberately replaces his mask. He has shown us his inner thoughts and feelings for the briefest time, then he replaces the mask which he wears constantly.'

This too helps articulate something which I'd been aware of in widescreen but not in close-up. The mask. The mask is everything to Burr. The image of himself which is presented to the world. The perception of oneself. The self-created personage which is presented is all anyone else in the story gets to see. Only two people see the deepest part: Alexander (somehow) and my confessor, the audience. All I show the world is all I show the world. Does Iago not leave Othello with the words, 'What you know, you know'?

MONDAY 11 DECEMBER

Nina.

Getting ready for the show there's a knock on my door.

'Yep?'
In the reflection of my mirror I see the door burst open and Lin bowls in.

'Yo!'
I turn my music down.
'Nina Simone! Cool. Hell of a way to get into the show.'

There's an album of hers I've listened to a lot. A live performance she gave at the Montreux Jazz Festival. The way she sings in that performance, utterly bare and exposed and raw and ferocious and tender and vulnerable. And yet there is massive self-confidence in it.

Lin and I chat. He looks up at some of the books I have on my shelf. Tells me which ones he found useful and which ones had nothing much in them.

It isn't a long conversation. It doesn't need to be. And he's doing the rounds before the show.

He has this childlike wonder about him. At the same time, his mind, like most brilliant artists I've encountered, is laser-sharp and multidirectional. He's that kid who ran up to you all and said: 'Guys!!!

I've just found the most amazing place down by the river! Come on!' And off you all go. He leads the adventure.

TUESDAY 12 DECEMBER

On my way into the theatre this morning I decided to pass by Westminster Cathedral. It's opposite the theatre. Westminster Abbey is older and more famous, but the cathedral is a sight to behold also. Massive and breathtaking inside, it's open most of the time to the public. Every once in a while when I'm in Victoria I'll go in for a moment. Well, now we're here.

As I got to the steps there was a homeless guy sitting there. It's bright but beyond freezing today. I put my hand in my pocket and gave him what change was in there, and he says, 'Thanks, brother. What you going in there for? Confess? What've you done then?' We both laugh.

'You're better off telling me. Least you can see me. What's the point of speaking to someone you can't see?'
'I think so that neither of you can judge the other.'
'He judges you, don't he? You make the confession and then he decides what you've got to do. Six Hail Marys or whatever. His only job sitting there is to judge.'

'True. I'm just going in to have a look around before work.'
'Fair enough.'

My hands were biting. I could only imagine what his felt like.

He said I didn't look like a businessman. By which I took him to mean that it's mostly office types working around here.

'I'm definitely not a businessman.'
'What do you do then, gym instructor? Actor?'
I laughed.
'He even laughs like an actor! We're all actors, though, I suppose. Don't think every one of them in that church ain't acting. What you in then?'

I told him and he proceeded to tell me that the American Revolution wasn't about freedom or liberty or tea, it was about the establishment of a bank.

I was a bit stunned. But then I've spoken to enough people living on the streets to know that if they've touched one extreme of society, they have very often touched the other. I asked him how he knew.

'Silly question. I had a bank account. My business to know. You could say it's in my interest. Why don't *you* know? Who d'you play then?'

I told him Aaron Burr. He didn't know who that was, so I found myself saying, 'Hamilton's friend.'

It felt strange hearing those words come out of my mouth.

'So you're playing a Yank then? Rebel. Fair enough. What've you got to say for yourself then? Never mind what I know, what do you know? We're all of us different, you know. All of us unique, you know that?'

He took my cold hand so the palm faced up.

'See that? Fingerprint. Every human being ever born or yet to be born has a completely unique fingerprint. No two alike. When you go to the airport, what do they do? Take that scan of your fingerprint. And your eye. Every human iris— completely unique and individual. Imagine that. Every human being utterly unique. You could search the globe and you'd never find another person with the same fingerprint, not your mother or father, identical twins. We're all of us perfectly unique, so what are you gonna do with yours . . . Mr Unique?'

WEDNESDAY 13 DECEMBER

Called at 12 to film the Electronic Press Kit on stage. This is done for most shows. Sequences of the show are filmed for the media to use for publicity. Somehow the day chosen always seems to come at the point when you're most tired. So. We get in costume and meet on stage. On the noticeboard the songs being filmed read:

'Opening'
'My Shot'
'Schuyler Sisters'
'Right Hand Man'
'You'll Be Back'
'Room Where It Happens'

Multiple cameras set up in the stalls. Some extra lighting. Band. Company. The works.

We go at it. As usual, everyone flinging themselves around the stage like ninja. Multiple takes of each song. Over and over. Adjustments. Camera angles. Between takes it's necking from water bottles and mopping down. Again, again, again.

By this stage in the rehearsal process, actors can give each other 'The Look' and communicate without words. After a couple of hours I began to see 'The Look' in the wings between takes. 'The Look' = 'They do know we have a show tonight, right?'

Then. After filming 'You'll Be Back' a bunch of times, Jibson's voice suddenly cracked on that high note. Everyone kind of froze. His voice is bulletproof. He got it together, but that's when it was clear how much everyone is trying to balance giving while trying not to burn out. Shin was saying she felt like she's fighting something. And Cleve. Next week are our final previews. You just want to hit opening week feeling fresh and fit.

Did 'Room' over and over and over until I found myself looking out into the auditorium and saying, 'This is the final time?' But there wasn't really a question mark on it. It went kind of quiet. We did that one and finished for the day.

Between filming and the show I nipped across the road to Pret in the station. As I came back I bumped into Westman on the rush-hour pavement opposite. Thousands of people swarming into Victoria Station and elbowing to get on buses, and we stood there as they all went by and we talked. We've both been thinking about fathers. Suddenly, question after question came pouring out. Questions about our own guy, about the other guy, some of which we could answer and some not: Do you think he felt this? Why do you think this matters to him? Why doesn't he do that? Do you think he ever thought this? Do you still feel the same way about this or that? Why, why why? Ended up standing there for forty-five mins.

When I got back to my dressing room the soup was stone-cold.

But the end of the show felt like fire.

THURSDAY 14 DECEMBER

Tommy gave a warning. Stay on it. We're getting it more in our bones now, but keep finding it.

We open exactly one week tonight. Feels like we are in good shape. Tired but we know what we are doing. We're getting better at steering the ship. I feel I am. Gradually.

After vocal warm-up was done, Beadle started playing 'Happy Birthday'. Everyone sang and they brought out a cake for me. This time a year ago I got the part. It's flown by, but at the same time seems a million years ago.

Then, between rehearsals and showtime, Jam, Obi, Rach and I went for food. I don't usually have big food at this point. It was taken as a victory that they'd managed to get me out. I felt like it today. Little place just round the corner. Of course, now it feels as if we have known each other all our lives. I love them.

FRIDAY 15 DECEMBER

In the interval last night, after 'Non-Stop', I felt that the whole thing reminds me of samurai stories I heard in Kyoto.

Brothers. Wars. Jealousy. Love. Betrayal. Revenge. Death.

I guess this story is from every culture you can imagine. From Cain and Abel, through Romulus and Remus, to *Star Wars*.

I see things about the show on Twitter now. I'm not on Insta or Facebook. But now every night I go home and see Twitter full of notifications. People seem to be enjoying it. But you have to be very careful about all that. We're still working. Hard not to look. I am vain enough to want to see the good, but not quite sturdy enough yet to ignore the bad.

Jam and I were talking about how we can get Black and Brown young people in to see the show. We have ideas. Could work.

SATURDAY 16 DECEMBER

For the average writer, words are abstract. For great writers, they are active. Lin is a great writer. Words are things—and when you breathe and receive his words, you feel this very clearly. We use words as a means of survival. Lin raps. And in rap every single word has its function. Its purpose. Every word can be a bomb. Designed, chosen and sent to have its impact. In hip hop, words cost—the speaker and the listener. Words are things. Not just ideas. Used correctly and in the right combinations they have a quality which goes beyond their intellectual value. Shakespeare knew and used this better than anyone, and Lin knows it too.

Consider the amount of songs in the show that are centred around the value and importance of words: 'One Last Time', 'Reynolds Pamphlet', 'Hurricane', 'Your Obedient Servant', 'Cab Battles #1 and 2', 'Farmer Refuted', 'Non-Stop', 'Yorktown' . . .

For instance. During the show tonight, I heard a line. One which I've heard many times before, but tonight—differently. On the way home it came back to me.

It comes during the song 'Burn'. Sung by Eliza after Hamilton's affair, the details of which he publishes in the Reynolds Pamphlet. Eliza sits alone with a lit lantern and all the letters Hamilton wrote to her— and she burns them. Her reaction to his infidelity is to want to erase herself from the narrative. During the song, while trying to fathom how her husband could betray her and make public the most personal details of their private lives, she has a line. One sentence. Eight words.

'The world has no place in our bed.'

On the most immediate level she is talking public versus private. The world—as in People, Society, the Public—have no right to know what happens in their private lives.

There is a beauty to how it is expressed. A poetry. 'The world has no place in our bed.'

But there is another level. Which is revealed if you look at the sentence literally. It's always interesting with language which is full of imagery to do this and see what it reveals.

Looking at the sentence, I see it deals with quantities of space: World. Place. Bed.

You can see what she's trying to say emotionally if you look at it literally: World. Place. Bed.

The largest physical space a human has contact with is the world. The globe. The planet. The smallest, a bed.

The world—a quantity of space big enough to fit all humans.
A bed—a quantity of space just enough to fit a human.

Imagine trying to fit the world into a bed.

Imagine trying to take the planet Earth, and cram it, force it, make it fit into a bed. Were it not a matter of love, it would be comical. But it is a matter of love.

A world cannot fit into a bed. It is an insane hope. And this is how insane Hamilton's behaviour must feel to Eliza. To her, the scale of his betrayal must seem planet-sized. To have this affair is one thing, to tell the world is another.

So Lin has Eliza illustrate her point by emphasising how it is not possible to fit vast into small. But he does so—and here's the genius—he does so by fitting these huge ideas and images into one tiny, monosyllabic, eight-word sentence. It takes just three seconds to say: 'The world has no place in our bed.'

It is one sentence in a song of many. Now, the audience is not going to sit there and ponder how big the Earth is. We sit and feel Eliza's pain. No, Lin is a poet and knows that words have many associations and resonances for us.

We can do both—if the writer knows his shit. We can feel what she is immediately feeling and we can also receive all the other information buried within her words.

This is why I like to call Lin 'the Alchemist'.

He knows that with language there is an intellectual sense, an emotional sense, and then there is this other thing. Something beyond both of these. He knows the maps and the routes and the recipes. Shakespeare knew them too.

If music be the food of love, play on.

SUNDAY 17 DECEMBER

'Non-Stop.'

Three times. Three times, Alexander asks Washington if he'd like him to run the Treasury or State department. Three times. And all I can do is stand there and wait. Wait to hear Washington's reply. In last night's performance I need less of my mind space to think about my next lyric/move than I did the night before. I am that bit freer than I was, to simply stand and listen and hear and watch and wait.

   – Treasury or State?
    Treasury or State?
    Sir, do you want me to run the Treasury or State
    department?
   – . . . Treasury.

And it eats me alive. I have never felt rage like that.

MONDAY 18 DECEMBER

I don't say anything in either Cabinet Battle but I hear everything.

★

Oskar Eustis was in tonight. From New York. Never met him before. He runs The Public Theater where the show started. He was dramaturg and co-director on *Angels in America*, among a million other things,

179

so to be standing in front of him meant more than I can say. He was so generous after. Especially about the duel and the ending. Went home happy.

WEDNESDAY 20 DECEMBER

'The World Was Wide Enough.'

I started out writing these entries whenever I could. Sometimes on the way into work, if the train wasn't too crowded. Sometimes if I could snatch a moment during the day. Now we're in the theatre it's on the way home or next morning. But I can never really remember about 'The World Was Wide Enough'. It's hard to talk about it. To remember it. The end of the show unfolds like a dream most nights.

Since we started running the show in rehearsals, then in performance, it's become the case that you work hard to tell the story, get the details right of the friendships and the war and the politics and the families and then . . . when you get to Weehawken, you breathe and let the thing loose and let it play out. The whole journey has been a kind of pulling-back of the trigger until finally, in the July dawn by the Hudson River, off it goes. However it might unfold in that moment, that run-through, that particular performance.

What is it to aim your gun at your friend? What is it to kill your brother? What is it to [*Unfinished line*]

The two of us—Hamilton and Burr—stand in that moment, pistols aimed at each other. I speak first, confessing to the audience how we'd 'rowed across the Hudson at dawn', building to the terrifying reiteration of the duel commandments:

Look him in the eye, aim no higher.
Summon all the courage you require.
Then count.

Alexander takes over with his version of events as I freeze, my pistol fixed straight at him. Well, time freezes. My mind and heart do not. It's more like that moment just before a car crashes. In that split second, your entire life is hyper-present. Choices. Regrets. Decisions. Mistakes. Some nights, like last night, I stand there looking at him beyond the end of the barrel of my pistol and feel in a way overtaken. That stillness can allow something powerful to occur. Aaron Burr is long dead, but in those moments, I am thinking and feeling and breathing on his behalf. He sees what I see and I feel what he felt. In some moments, for fleeting flashes, I am him.

Jam and I don't really speak about this moment too conclusively. It shouldn't be pinned down. I guess we've both ventured into our own individual caves to face it. He doesn't need to know my thoughts on it, and I don't need to know his. It's enough to look in his eyes.

I suspect that after that fateful day, Burr had to relive it every day for the rest of his life. Not a day went by when it wasn't replayed in his mind. I imagine him every evening forced to relive the drama called 'Hamilton' all over again. Scouring every detail, every syllable, every comma, for the defining moment where it all went wrong. When was it? When he was orphaned? When he decided to turn his back on his father's theology? When he met Alexander? When he refused Alexander's offer to join him in writing the Federalist Papers? When he unseated Hamilton's father-in-law Philip Schuyler? When he refused to give Alexander a definitive answer to his plea for help at the end of 'We Know', telling him instead: 'Alexander, rumors only grow. And we both know what we know'?

What if? What if either of them had done things differently, would we be at Weehawken at all? Would Burr be the so-called villain? Did he have a choice? If he didn't, then how can you vilify him? And even if he did, how can you blame him?

And so, in a way, each song he tells is an exploration of a moment where the story *could* have gone a different way. What if he hadn't met Alexander that day? What if Alexander hadn't stopped him? What if Angelica hadn't brushed him off? What if Washington had promoted him? What if they'd lost the war? What if he'd won the election? What if Alexander hadn't . . . ? But he did. He did. And what if Burr hadn't needed to demand satisfaction? Burr might be looking down the barrel at Hamilton, but he is also aiming at himself.

So you walk out on stage every night and lay it all out for your confessors one last time in the hope that tonight, maybe, just maybe it might go another way.

I discussed this with Tommy one day in rehearsals. 'Right,' he said. 'When Burr walks out there at the top, maybe tonight it will be different. Maybe this time he tells the story, it will have a different ending.'

The very first thing I tell our audience is that 'I'm the damn fool that shot him.' And yet, if we do our job properly, by the end of the night, when we walk out for the duel at Weehawken, they, like us, shouldn't know which way it's going to go.

At Weehawken, Burr tells us that the doctor required to be present at duels 'turned around so he could have deniability'. But in the musical version of the story, the audience is not permitted this escape. Burr forces them to see the whole thing. Making them complicit. I deny them deniability. And my final word as the trigger is pulled becomes theirs:

WAIT!

Silence.

I felt last night that the audience was as shocked as I was.

I should've known.

Then a repeat. The second gotta mean something different from the first.

> I should've known
> The world was wide enough for both Hamilton
> and me.

There are two brief moments, both historically accurate details that I'm glad Lin and Tommy kept in.

After the pistol is fired and its bullet hits Alexander 'right between his ribs', 'I walk towards him, but I am ushered away'.

Burr did approach Hamilton, and scholars debate what it was that he wanted to say. Last night I knew exactly what I wanted to say. But as the oarsmen 'row him back across the Hudson', it hits me right between the ribs that I am not permitted to say it.

Instead, 'I get a drink.' (Is it the same drink in the same tavern where we first met?) As always, it's the detail. The specificity of the character trying to get the details exactly right. It's not about emotion, it is about clarity. I must make you understand exactly what happened.

See, I'm not here to tell myself the story. I know the story. My confidants, the audience, don't. My emotion in the scene isn't as important as the audience's understanding. Focus on telling them the details. Don't get swept up in the emotion.

And then there's the other moment, as I face the audience and tell them:

> They say
> Angelica and Eliza–
> Were both at his side when he died.

Meaning. That they were there. In the room.

And I. At the last. When it mattered most.

Was not.

THURSDAY 21 DECEMBER

Opening night.

You get up. Go to the gym. Run. Always running. Turn around and think: Christ, it looks a long way down to the foot of this mountain. In the distance, trees and people are dots. It's been a long time running. Chasing. Searching. Trying. Looking. Burning. You check your voice. Always. Well, now it's too late. It's all there or it isn't. Texts all morning: 'Good Luck.' 'Break a leg tonight.' 'I'm so proud of you.' 'Enjoy.'

Enjoy?

Well, joy certainly.

On the mid-morning train platform. Cold. Clear. Grey sky but bright. Christmas is everywhere. How did that happen? Train empty. I look up and, at the end of the carriage, a poster: '*HAMILTON.*' Pull into Blackheath Station and on the opposite platform a bigger poster: '*HAMILTON.*'

I stop looking at my phone. Then the city looms into view. It's so cold that they've left the train heating on full whack. The carriage is boiling. My homeless mate will not be so warm right now. The train stops. On the tracks. Signals. We wait. And wait. I stare out of the window. London. Massive and out there. Concrete and steel and glass and brick.

What a time.

I'm in early to get first-night cards for everyone. Theatre is nothing if not its rituals.

The company are addicted to Nando's. Leslie and Johnny and Jack and Barney and the guys plan their days around the place. There's one just up from the theatre. As a present I get everyone a Nando's gift card with enough for a couple of meals on it.

The two things which have powered this company: Laughter and Protein.

Text Jam.

We are allowed two tickets each for the show tonight. But Katy lets me have four. My three sisters are coming and my niece Malaika. I have booked them into a hotel near the theatre for tonight so they can enjoy the party. We have a show tomorrow and two Saturday, so I will be in my bed by 1 a.m. latest. But they can swig till the booze dries up. The party is at the theatre. Not sure why it's not at one of those big swanky bars somewhere. But hey.

Note to self: remember to get 'Like I said' right in 'Aaron Burr, Sir'.

Come into Soho and pick up cards. At the theatre. Flowers already. I can tell the ones from Mark straight away. I wish he was here. Cards. Gifts. Check on the sisters. Coming down after work. They haven't seen the show yet. The kids all know the songs by heart.

I wish my mother were here to see it too.

She taught me to sing. And dance. And go out and see the world.

The only time she ever said anything explicitly about my voice was only a few years ago. The eldest cousin in our family passed away in Barbados. My mother was only a couple of years older than her, being the seventh child of eight. Mum was sick so couldn't go back to Barbados for the funeral. So I went. When I came back I went straight and told her how it had gone. The big church under the Caribbean sun full of family and friends from all over the island. I told her what passages were read and what hymns sung.

'And did you sing?'
'No.'
'Why not? You have such a sweet voice.'

Writing cards can be tricky. Not with this group. I
sit down here in the dressing room and it is easy to
know what to write. It is only pride and admiration
and love which bubbles up. I said that we'd only get
through it together and it was true. I have seen them
smile and cry and struggle and fall and get back up
and silently face many dragons. It is not ultimately
for Steph or Andy or Tommy or Lac or Lin that
that arm or that note or that thought needs to be
right. It is for something within us. Some contract
we made long ago with whichever god gave us our
talent. If it is not right then we know first. I have
seen my brothers and sisters wrestle with all kinds
of moments. Some publicly, most privately. In
corners of rehearsals rooms, in the darkness of the
wings. I have seen them do wonders of physics-
ography. Create shapes and sing notes on stage
which are hard to explain. I have heard them laugh
and encourage each other and—step by step, day by
day—we have pulled each other up the face of this
mountain. Moment by moment, bar by bar, note by
note, thought by thought, button by button, stitch
by stitch. I have seen them low and desperate and
before they can reach out a hand for help, a hand or
a smile or a joke has been there to pull them up.
I have seen them want to be good not just for
themselves, but for each other.

One afternoon in rehearsal I remember we all collapsed into a heap on top of and within each other. We had just completed staging something. And all that was left was to heap on the floor in the middle of the revolve. Like a tangle of snakes. A creature with many limbs and many laughing heads. Not sure whose arm your head was resting on or whose leg was on your arm. Unplanned and un-led. There we were. The Americans and stage management stood wonder-faced and smiling, but at that moment, it was what we needed. And so we laughed and tickled each other and breathed out and allowed ourselves to acknowledge that we were one thing. One group. I have been inspired by them and have tried to inspire.

Knock on the door. Tommy. I had initially thought that his silence during auditions meant that he wasn't interested in me for this part. Then I came to see that he just knew what he saw. Likewise in rehearsals. He lets me go. Trusts me. I see that now. When I need gathering in, he will do so. I see that he sees that the only way to come to this part (or any part) is to stagger in the dark, bump into things, dare to go forward, reach, see without seeing.

'How you doing, buddy?' Asks about my sisters. We are both close to our sisters.

He says that at the curtain call after the show there are going to be speeches. He asks if I will introduce everybody to the audience. First the cast, then we'll be joined on stage by the offstage company, our swing bros and sisters. Then the creative team—Steph, Andy, Lac, Paul, Nevin, Ron Chernow, Tom himself—and then he'll introduce Lin.

That's something else I have to remember.

We all gather on stage and Tommy speaks. The energy in the space is buzzing.

Tell the story.

Everywhere you look, you behold an exhausted smile. Everyone has family in tonight. For the first time it is not only for ourselves and our team, but also for the people who went without just so that we could be here. Who went without so that someone could go to dance classes or singing lessons.

I look out into the auditorium. The tech tables and laptops are gone. Now just seats. Cameron's beautiful auditorium. Somehow it's built. Each light bulb, every figure on the ceiling, each brushstroke, each button, every cuff, every stitch in its rightful place.

I stand and breathe as people leave the stage to go and do their thing. When it is empty, now I am alone. I see Lin at the back. He goes. Now, only a sea of seats. Green. The colour of money. The colour of envy. The colour of life. The colour of mountains. When I face these seats again they will be occupied. My confessors. My confidants. Friends. The only ones I trust. Will they believe me tonight? Will they understand what leads me to the trigger? We shall see. If I do my job right, they might.

Stand. Breathe. Look. Try to empty my mind.

Somehow, for some reason, I have been brought to this place to tell this story, now. So tell it. That's all.

As I leave the stage, it is gratitude. To all the hands that have guided me here. To those brothers and sisters in NY who made this thing to begin with. I see Chris Jackson's smile.

You pass people scurrying up stairwells and corridors, sliding cards under doors and leaving gifts against doorframes. Over the tannoy you hear, 'Miss So-and-So—a package has just been dropped off for you at stage door.'

I come to my dressing room. Quiet. Silence.

Just before the half. Knock. Cameron. It was he who first said, 'This guy should play Burr.' Before I even knew what *Hamilton* was. I haven't spoken to him backstage once since we've been at the theatre. Only out front. He's been busy building. And yet here he is in my dressing room. He very quietly and with a smile of concentration I've not seen on him before says only a few things, but they pierce me. He talks just a few sentences about Burr, without ever saying the word 'Burr'. I am a little surprised to find myself listening to Cameron Mackintosh speak so delicately about relationships, but this journey is nothing if not a wonder. He does not talk of Barricades or Chandeliers or Helicopters, he speaks of how there is a certain kind of hurt we feel which can only be caused by those who love us the most. Wishes me break a leg and then he is gone. Leaving me moved. The conversation happens so quickly and my spirit is just starting to dip its foot in the shores of Outer Body that I don't try to process what Cameron has just said. I just know that he is right and let his words dissolve into me.

Music.

Nina Simone—'Feelings'. Dylan. *Tosca*—Tito Gobbi. Wainwright—'Dinner at Eight'.

'Ladies and gentlemen of the *Hamilton* company, this is your half-hour call. Half an hour, please.'

I go to see Jam. His table full of cards. Flowers. He seems pretty good. Calm. Time for a few last-minute jokes and some of Bonham Carter's tea. The little waiting room between our two dressing rooms has somehow been christened 'Weehawken'. The company will meet in there to chat or hang out or discuss things. So here we are now. What is it like in his shoes? Someone said he has big shoes to fill. But he's six foot four. His feet are massive. He has more talent, more mind and more heart than anyone I've ever met. I start to say so, but it doesn't really come out. We both understand. It's never really been about words. Both know what we have to do.

'Fuck 'em up, bro.'
'Fuck 'em up.'

At beginners' call, every night, those of us who start in the stage-right wing gather and put our arms round each other's shoulders, and someone will lead a prayer as the last of the audience settles. Usually Our Sister Beloved, Rachel. Even Jibson, who isn't called at beginners, will come down and join this moment with us.

Sometimes it starts a little too close to the house lights going down, so I'll have to duck out early. I need that moment on my own. But tonight we are there in good time. Thankful. Grateful. Happy. With someone's arm around your shoulder. Glad of each other. Those of us who don't even pray to any god are glad to join in some thanks. God or no god, *something* has brought us together. Some force has made it so that we are stood here holding each other in the darkness of the stage-right wing of the Victoria Palace Theatre. Tired and energised. Burnt out and full of fire. Exhausted and excited. Proud and free. Leaning on each other and pulling each other up. We pray for strength and safety and joy. Strength to lift and support each other, to have fun, to tell the story. Jam and I squeeze each other's shoulder.

It is a fizzing energy backstage. Get that last bit of fizz out. For we know that when we step out onto that stage, it's only warriors.

Every night at this point I've found myself doing this one thing. At the furthest upstage-right entrance in the wings there are some steps leading up to the top level of our stage set. The steps start in the wing, but by the time you reach the top of them you are on stage. Just before I stand in my position to start the show, I go up those steps, nearly to the top. From there, if I am stealthy, I can peek and see a fragment of the audience. A little peephole to the Royal Circle. As the audience are taking their seats I can spy them. The last few nights I go up there just before we start. I spend the show speaking to the audience, but during the show you can only see some of them, the first few rows of each level. So I take this moment to look and see who we are telling the story to. Find someone. Some face. Some young person or some parent. Someone. See their eyes. So that in my mind's eye I know who it is I am talking to throughout the show. I am not just talking to a void, I am talking *to* someone. Much depends on it. They are not observers, they are participants. Witnesses. Tonight it is this little Black girl. Maybe ten years old. Sat between her mum and dad. Plaits. The look on her face. So excited. Eyes wide and full of joy and wonder and excitement. Like she can hardly believe she is finally getting to see *Hamilton*. Like she can't believe she's here.

Well, neither can I. It is that same look I felt when I first put the CD in the player and heard the mighty Leslie Odom Jr. say 'How does a . . . ' The same look I had when I first sat in the Richard

Rodgers Theatre and saw *Hamilton: An American Musical*. The same feeling I had when I staggered out of that same theatre at intermission onto the high-summer sidewalk of Broadway. The same feeling I had running back up Eighth Avenue after my audition. The same feeling I had when my agent rang on my birthday last year and said, 'We'll have an offer in the morning.' The same feeling I had on day one of rehearsals when we all sat down and my brother started singing 'My Shot'. The same feeling when we all sang the show through for the first time and behind me I heard all of us sing as one, 'Who lives, who dies, who tells your story?'

And as I look out, I realise that that same feeling I see in that little girl's eyes is in my eyes too. So I go stand in my spot. In the dark. Waiting for my cue light to go green. I hear the audience's excited static noise. It fades as I close my eyes quickly and thank all those who have helped me to get here. Those alive and those long gone. Ask them to come with me now. I need you. In my mind's eye I see Tommy sitting quietly in the stalls, arms folded. He'll know I'm standing here. I always am. I feel him say silently to me: 'Just do what you do. Tell the story. I believe in you.'

A voice from behind me whispers: 'That's front-of-house clearance. Are you happy, Mr Terera?' I nod. Across the stage in the opposite wing I see Jason Pennycooke. He thumbs-up. I blow a kiss. The houselights start to go down. Jibson's King George public announcement starts to play. In my mind I can see Lac giving me the nod: 'Okay?' My soul nods back. See my cue light turn from red to green. The colour of money. The colour of envy. Of life. Mountains. And I realise that I'm here. I've reached. I made it. It's been . . . somehow it happened. You don't climb mountains by the mile or by X thousand feet, you go one step at a time. One foot in front of the other. Until finally you look up and you're there. Then all that's left to do is empty your lungs, your mind and your soul, let the breath drop in. And step.

As Lin's iconic chords ring out.

BUM! BUH BUH BUH BUH BUH BUH!

Turn to face the audience, my confessors, my confidants, my friends, and ask: 'How?'

The view is . . . sweet.

PART FIVE

AFTERWARDS

We opened the show.

And suddenly our little gang of thirty or so exploded, and we noticed that the whole world seemed to be staring at us. The work up to that point had been so intense that we hadn't really had time to think about what was going on outside the rehearsal room. All our focus had been on getting that harmony right in 'Quiet Uptown', mastering that step in 'My Shot'. Suddenly there were hundreds of people outside the theatre, things in the press every day, people stopping you in the street, a social-media fest, each week famous people in the audience and backstage. The Rock one night, Peter Brook the next, Prince Harry and Meghan.

Yet the thing I found most fascinating still remained this character, his journey and the story. You learn only so much throughout rehearsals. Those first weeks are just the beginning. You learn what a story truly is, who a character is, by performing night after night. Looking back now, it's interesting to see how much my thoughts and feelings evolved. Not only was I playing this character, I was being taught by him.

You see, in the theatre there is a kind of duel which takes place between the actor and the character. No shots are fired. Duels are not tests of strength, they are tests of character.

The actor and character must meet. One cannot function without the other. One cannot be afraid of the other. They must challenge each other and dare each other to action. They must look each other in the eye. Pay the closest attention to every detail. The actor must challenge the character not to hold back, and the character must challenge the actor to do the same. Bravery is required. The stakes could not be higher. At any moment, one could perhaps dominate the other, but then the thing would be over. What is required is balance. That moment. When both are thinking, feeling, moving as one. When neither is really leading. When both are each other's obedient servant. When both stand in the clear dawn air and for a moment, even the briefest of moments, are as alive as it is possible to be.

★

So. The roller coaster sped on through spring into summer. If rehearsals are the sprint, performance is the marathon. Stamina and focus are the skills needed in order to keep the performance fresh so that familiarity is not allowed to breed contempt.

The story must be newly discovered each night, regardless of who's in the audience. The same commitment given on a wet Thursday matinee in September as on the opening night nine months earlier. With *Hamilton* we were helped in this task. Every single night there was a gassed-up, hungry audience waiting for it, who were so ready to hear this story and go on a journey, that never once did it feel the same as the night before.

So we grew as the year unfolded. But I found myself writing less in my journal. Perhaps there was more time now to experience the experience.

Two memories stand out that contain the essence of the whole experience for me. One on stage, one off.

★

Shortly after we opened it was time for the annual Olivier Awards ceremony, held at the Royal Albert Hall. We found out that we would be performing. Opening the show in fact. Exciting because this would be the first time we'd be seen outside of the theatre.

We rehearsed in late March. It was the first time we'd seen the American creatives since we'd opened. As usual, Tommy poked his head around the corner at company warm-up and everyone went crazy. We were told that the song we'd be performing was the opening number, 'Alexander Hamilton'. Which everyone was gassed about. Except me. I gulped. I was guessing they might want us to do 'Schuyler Sisters' or 'Yorktown' maybe, like at the Tony Awards in New York. But no. 'Alexander Hamilton' it was to be. So not only would we be starting the whole ceremony, but I'd be walking out to begin it. On my own.

The week before the ceremony we spent a couple of afternoons rehearsing at the Victoria Palace. The reason it took a lot of rehearsing is the reason why I ultimately enjoyed the day so much. It had been decided that the entire company would perform in the number, including swings and covers. Let me explain. In the company, there is the onstage cast who perform the show every night, and then we have other members of our cast called swings and standbys, who are backstage every night. When someone is sick or on holiday, the swing steps in to perform that part. This is necessary in a musical because of the crazy logistics of such large productions. When a show is rehearsed, we all learn the show together, and then throughout the year, due to holidays and illness, constant casting variations occur each week. It's always exciting when a cover goes on to play a part for the first time.

At the Oliviers, though, for the only time during the run, the opening number was going to be staged and performed including our entire cast. All on stage at the same time.

We rehearsed hard. It was exciting, but also a little funky to have a stage full of people during the number. The stage at the Albert Hall would be enormous, so thirty actors would feel great. But on our stage it made us all giddy. Same stage. Same song. Just twice as many bodies. Extra moves and traffic had to be thought up. Complementary bits of staging and choreography given to people. As so often happened during the *Hamilton* experience, it was a kind of zany, last-day-of-the-school-year atmosphere. Everyone excited and buzzing. And Steph trying to maintain order and get the thing staged. Herding cats. Joy.

The day of the ceremony came and was pretty intense from the git-go. Early start at the Albert Hall. Many of the other shows in the West End were also going to be performing, and each production had their designated slot to rehearse and soundcheck on the huge stage throughout the day. Ours was around 10 a.m. The day was so packed that thankfully there wasn't a lot of time to think about how nervous we were.

It went something like this.

Arrive. Find the dressing room. Get into mics with the sound team. Go up to the stage. Soundcheck all the mics and sound. Stage the number. Rehearse it and run it a bunch of times. Get back out of mics. Back to the dressing room. Grab a bite. Get into your fancy clothes in order to go and do the official red carpet with its interviews and photographs. Back to the dressing room to get out of fancy clothes. Get into show costumes, hair and make-up and mics. Get taken up to position for the start of the show. Perform the opening of the show. Back to the dressing room as the ceremony carries on. Out of costume and mics. Back into fancy clothes. Go back into the auditorium to rejoin the ceremony and wait for your category. Party. Bed.

Fast.

The reason why I'm telling this story is because of something which happened in the middle of that whirlwind day.

We'd all been outside for the red carpet and were now backstage in the dressing rooms, getting into show costumes for the start of the ceremony and our performance itself. They had us in these large rooms in the bowels of the place, sharing with a couple of the other shows. Men in one large room, ladies in the one next door. It was great to see friends from the other casts.

Once we were all in costume, ready and waiting to get called up to the stage to perform, I called the ladies into our room so that we could have the little shared moment we liked to have before each show back at the theatre. A moment where we all got to connect with each other and give thanks for what we were about to do. Only this moment was different. Usually at the theatre half the cast is on one side of the stage to start the show and the other half starts on the opposite side of the stage. We never get to be together. Here at the Albert Hall we were all together and about to do the thing. All costumed up and ready to go. Five thousand people waiting up there and countless more watching on television at home. Waiting to see, hear, encourage, compare. We were just happy. Not a lot was said in any official capacity. We just took a moment to be together. Jam spoke some words. Gave some jokes. And then suddenly, from nowhere, someone began to sing. 'Amazing Grace'. I think it was Rachel. It just rang out. Then someone else's voice joined hers. Two voices. Then someone else and someone else, until before long it was all of us singing. Harmonies. More harmonies. Layers. Counters. Groups. Riffs. Pairings. Rhythms. Volumes. *Hamilton* choir in the belly of the Albert Hall! The room was ringing with voices singing. It was the quality of the sound. It rose and cascaded and rang out. Deafening. No one really led it or drew it to a close. It sort of just happened. All of us contributed to it. And afterwards we went up and opened the show. It was one of the most powerful moments I've ever experienced. Something within those few seconds encapsulated what I value so much about the *Hamilton* experience—and theatre as an art form. Some spark occurs, takes on some beautiful life of its own, is intensely powerful, is felt by everyone who witnesses it, and then, as quickly as it came, is gone. Leaving its impression on your soul.

★

When *Hamilton* opened on Broadway, the experience of walking into a New York theatre and seeing the Founding Fathers and Mothers portrayed by actors of colour sent vibrations through America. More so because, at that very moment, little Black girls were growing up in the White House. Revolutionary moments.

When it first opened, no one knew the show. Hip hop was as unfamiliar to Broadway audiences as Alexander Hamilton was. The impact of what that audience was witnessing was seismic.

We wanted to know: what was our British equivalent?

I wanted to know how our telling of this story could carry that same sense of boldness and achieve what theatre always seeks, but doesn't always reach—a true reflection of the times. The greatest theatre illuminates both the time in which it's set and the time in which it's performed. How could we achieve that when, by the time the play had landed on British shores, it seemed as if the entire planet knew every word of every song? Familiar as Mickey Mouse.

My twin sister had brought my niece and nephew, Gaby and Jude, many times to see the show. They were both obsessed with every song and character. One day she sent me a text with lots of laughing emojis.

She said she was watching the news on TV, and Jude was on the floor, colouring. The reporter was talking about America, how Barack Obama was America's first Black president, and without missing a beat Jude looked up and said very simply, 'No he wasn't . . . George Washington was.'

That's how powerful theatre can be.

How could we make the experience have as powerful an impact in the UK as it did in America? Jam and I would sit in our dressing rooms before the show and discuss this a lot. We all did. Obi and Jason and Waylon and Tarinn and Rachel and Christine and Jibson, the whole cast would get deep into discussion. What can we do?

As actors we were acutely aware of the issues our own society faces. Issues of inequality, prejudice, racism, disempowerment. We'd always come back to the central question of the piece: Who lives, who dies, who tells your story?

What is *our* story?

In New York, the production had run a beautiful educational programme alongside the show which they called EduHam. They would have workshops and classes and performances of the show for schoolchildren and students from all over the country. Encouraging them to learn, create, take ownership. Once the show was up and running in the UK, we were looking forward to creating something similar. A programme which could use this experience to inspire and unlock potential in a young, hungry generation who in *Hamilton* had found theatre which spoke directly to their lives.

It proved trickier than expected to make a reality. Until one day in late summer, Jam and I were at a charity football match that had been organised by a friend in aid of the survivors and community of the Grenfell Tower fire. We sat and once again found ourselves asking the question: What are we doing? What can we do? I said, 'It'll be winter before we know it. The contract will finish. People'll leave the cast. Even if it were just one show with young people, that would be something.' Jam, always ready to leap first and ask questions later, said, 'Let's do it. Once we get something going it'll be easier to build on.' We sat as goals were scored on the pitch and goals were pursued in our minds. We were trying to work out how we could make something happen before the end of the year while all our original cast were still together. We decided that we had to reach out to Lin and Tommy and tell them this was something we had to do. We drafted a letter and next day sent it to them both. A meeting was set up with the producers, and within a couple of weeks we had an extra performance scheduled specifically for young people from schools from all over the UK. A Tuesday matinee. The cast all got on board and we all came up with a list of schools we'd attended and schools we'd heard of from areas that might not have access to expensive West End theatre. It was a start. It was something.

The day of the show came. Coachloads turned up. Some having set out early from the other end of the country to get here. The cast met on stage to warm up as usual and we were already pretty emotional then. Looking out and seeing all the programmes placed on every seat. The atmosphere of anticipation in the auditorium was utterly different from anything we'd experienced so far. We stood in our group circle on stage and whoever needed to speak spoke. As we got into costume and prepared in our dressing rooms, over the tannoy you could hear the auditorium filling up. Groups of twenty or thirty from each school. The noise grew. These young people were fired up.

Then it was time to do it.

It's hard to describe what took place in that theatre that afternoon. I can only think back and shake my head. Fifteen hundred young people from all backgrounds, all colours, all classes, receiving and claiming the show in a way totally different from the audiences we had in the evenings. As young people, different things spoke to them. They reacted and responded to different moments, different thoughts, lyrics. Different characters. They heard different things. Laughed at different things. To them it wasn't a history lesson, it was about them.

During the opening number there is a moment—on the line 'You never learned to take your . . . time!'—when the whole cast lines up across the front of the stage. When we stand and face the audience. See their faces. This day it was a sea of Black and Brown and White faces. It was a mirror. For the first time we fully saw ourselves out there, and our audience saw themselves up on the stage. It is not possible to convey what that moment felt like or what it meant. But all I can say is that when Shakespeare has Hamlet say that in theatre we must 'hold, as 'twere, the mirror up to nature', I got it more deeply that day than I'd ever understood it before.

We saw young people in that auditorium see themselves. We saw it. And what they were seeing were leaders and thinkers and achievers. They were seeing possibility. When Tarinn came out as Hercules Mulligan, it was them. That's how they express. When he bowled onto the stage, the place came apart. When Washington wrestled with how to win as the underdog, they encouraged him. They had no patience with Burr, they were with Laurens and the Sons of Liberty all the way—let's get on with it! Rise up! Change the world! When Philip wanted to make his father proud, they got it. When Eliza burned the letters, they were with her. And the sound! Deafening. The silences too. They breathed with us. They were utterly present and involved—and the story was theirs.

After it was done, the young people stayed in the auditorium, while we got changed out of costume quickly, came back on stage, and we all had a Q&A discussion which lasted about forty-five emotionally charged minutes.

During it, Obi spoke very simply and directly and quietly with them: 'This is less about us and more about you. What's your story? What do you want to express? What is your experience? What is the story of your life? You Lin-Manuels sitting out there, what is the story you want to tell? What is your Yorktown? Your shot that you are not going to throw away?'

As they left the auditorium, it seemed like those young people, maybe they walked a little taller. I know *we* all did.

That performance, that afternoon, that moment held within it the essence of the *Hamilton* experience for me . . .

Who lives? Who dies? Who tells *your* story?

CODA

One final true story from research. An actual exchange I found between Burr and a woman who was his landlady. The words are theirs, but I've imagined the scene.

★

And so, in his old-man days, Burr found himself the villain in everyone's history. Despised. Outcast. Alone. Until, fed up of being on the run around Europe and South America, he chose to return to New York. Spending his final months in a boarding house in the downtown area he'd once ruled. One morning there is the usual knock at his door. The landlady knows that there is rarely an answer nowadays, not because the old man's hearing has gone but because his care has. After a respectful pause she enters with the breakfast tray.

'Colonel Burr, what do you think I heard this morning? They say in the whispers that I am your mistress.'

Bringing his face from the window. 'Well, we don't care for that, do we?'

'Not a bit, but they say something else—that I am your daughter!'

'Do they?' Turning back to the window and the grey Hudson beyond it.

'I don't think we care much for that, do we?' Then a pause.

'Well, I'll tell you this, here's something they might say that would be true: She gave the old man a home when no one else would.'

ILLUSTRATIONS

REHEARSAL

After page 64

Rehearsals at Jerwood Space. The room was always full of our cast using every second to practise. You can also see the revolve or turntable in some shots. The first number in the show to feature it is 'The Schuyler Sisters'. Before we staged the number we practised getting on and off it as it turned. For me it's a good metaphor for *Hamilton*, and also life—when you step on, you have to commit to the direction you are going in, or you might fall. Another photo shows our choreographer Andy Blankenbuehler giving great insights and our director Tommy Kail, always guiding.

Page 1–3: All photos by Matt Crockett, courtesy of Dewynters.

Page 4: All photos courtesy of Giles Terera, except photo of the Victoria Palace Theatre (bottom centre) © Cameron Mackintosh Limited.

★

PERFORMANCE

After page 112

It was a very special moment on the first day of tech when we all saw each other in our new clothes for the first time. The detail of which, sometimes unseen by the audience, always fascinated me. One thing. The photo where I'm standing behind the chair is taken during the song 'Dear Theodosia'. You can see the wedding ring, which I've just put on during the costume change before the number. It's a tiny detail which is never mentioned or referred to, but which represents a massive shift in the character. Everything means something.

Page 1: (*top*) *'Aaron Burr, Sir' with Jamael Westman;* (*bottom*) *'The Schuyler Sisters' with Rachelle Ann Go, Rachel John and Christine Allado.*

Page 2: (*clockwise from top left*) *'Dear Theodosia'; 'Non-Stop' with Jamael Westman; 'Wait for It'; 'Washington on Your Side' with Jason Pennycooke.*

Page 3: (*top*) *'The Room Where It Happens' with Leah Hill, Jack Butterworth, Curtis Angus, Jason Pennycooke, Miriam-Teak Lee, Waylon Jacobs, Tarinn Callender, Obioma Ugoala, Leslie Garcia Bowman, Courtney-Mae Briggs, Cleve September, Johnny Bishop and Kelly Downing;* (*bottom*) *'The Room Where It Happens' with Kelly Downing, Rachel John, Jack Butterworth, Curtis Angus, Miriam-Teak Lee, Johnny Bishop, Leslie Garcia Bowman and Obioma Ugoala.*

Page 4: (*top*) *'Your Obedient Servant'*; (*bottom*) *'The World Was Wide Enough' with Jamael Westman in the background.*

All photos by Matthew Murphy © George III Productions Limited.

★

BEHIND THE SCENES

After page 160

These photos give you a look at what life was like on 'Planet *Hamilton*', including the opening night, with me introducing our company and creative team onto the stage. The central pages are a montage of photos from my phone, showing backstage moments with this amazing company, including with our Founding Father, Lin-Manuel Miranda. The final page shows the Royal gala in aid of Sentebale, in August 2018 (when Prince Harry kicked off his speech singing a few words of his great-great-great-great-great-great grandfather's song), and me on stage at the Oliviers at the Royal Albert Hall.

Page 1: (top) by Matthew Murphy © George III Productions Limited; (bottom) by David M. Benett/Getty Images Entertainment via Getty Images.

Pages 2 & 3: All photos courtesy of Giles Terera.

*Page 4: (top) by Dan Charity/*The Sun *via PA Images/Alamy Stock Photo; (bottom) by Jeff Spicer/Getty Images Entertainment via Getty Images.*

★

Photos and journal extracts on pages 28, 42, 130, 152 & 198: All courtesy of Giles Terera.

Cover photo by Matthew Murphy © George III Productions Limited; Author photo by Graham Michael.

ACKNOWLEDGEMENTS

Thanks to my literary agent, Kara Fitzpatrick. My editor, Matt Applewhite. My agent, Simon Beresford. Trevor Jackson, Fabi Waisbort, Jeffrey Seller, Jolyon Coy, Alex Waldmann, Leigh Macdonald.

Special thanks to Thomas Kail, Lin-Manuel Miranda, Jamael Westman, Mark Dugdale, my sisters, Tarinda Terera, Farayi Agbame and Nikki Austin, Alec and Bobby Poole, and Dan Poole.